D0902168

Nobody Owns Me

A Celibate Woman Discovers Her Sexual Power

A Narrative Journal
By Francis B. Rothluebber

San Diego, California

LuraMedia™

Publisher's Catalog Number LM647
Printed and Bound in the United States of America

Cover image by Sara Steele.
" Vuylstekeara Cambria 'Plush' " © 1984 by Sara Steele, All Rights Reserved.
Collection of Charles N.K. Cluxton.
Cover design by Tom Jackson, Philadelphia.

LuraMedia, Inc.
7060 Miramar Road, Suite 104
San Diego, California 92121

Library of Congress Cataloging-in-Publication Data
Rothluebber, Francis B., date.
Nobody owns me : a celibate woman discovers her sexual power / by Francis B. Rothluebber.
p. cm.
ISBN 1-880913-13-5
1. Sex—Religious aspects—Christianity. 2. Feminism—Religious aspects—Christianity. 3. Women—Religious life. 4. Femininity (Psychology). I. Title.
BT708.R64 1994
248.4'7—dc20 94-6154
CIP

Grateful acknowledgment is made for permission to reprint quotations from *Wisdoms* by Dorothy Maclean. Published in 1971 by Findhorn Foundation, Forres, Scotland. Second Edition in 1979. Reprint in 1991 by Colombiere Center, Box 676, Idyllwild, California 92549.

Introductory Note

I offer this brief explanation before you start to read this journal. The woman who wrote herself alive in writing these pages never intended this journal be published. She sent her journal to me some months ago as a thank you for the experiences we had shared.

I found that the sentences kept returning to my mind. As I met with others, I often wished I could share parts of the journal with them. I thought the experiences could encourage and support their struggle to become who they really are.

The writer agreed to let her writing be printed. We changed names and places, but everything else is just as she journaled.

— *Dr. Iris Clayton*

Monday, July 20 – Morning

Nothing special today, I thought as I awoke. The sheet was already sticking to me. When I threw it back, the familiar gray stone fell into the pit of my stomach. This was *not* an ordinary day. All the while I showered and listened to the coffee sounds, the argument went on: I really don't have to see this woman. She sounded so secure on the phone. Dr. Iris Clayton. Iris. Her mother must have picked the name from a Southern novel. I need to keep remembering that Bert, my worried friend, said she'd heard Dr. Clayton was good, very good. I will go. I have to get this whole thing settled once and for all.

I've taken all the pages out of my binder and put in a new pack of loose-leaf. The old heap is finished. Fallen into the sere, the yellow leaf, as Shakespeare says. I guess those pages brought me to this moment.

Anyway, I'm starting with this new journal pad. It's a promise to myself: I will go to see her. At least see what she's like. No, see whether I can trust her. If not, I'll give her my check, thank her, and leave.

I need to get going, stop in at my desk first, take the messages off the machine, if there are any, and let Jane know I'll be out. She'll look at me as she has lately, with her questioning eyes. 'What are you doing to earn your salary in this parish?' Surviving, honey, surviving.

Strange, I feel dread and I feel excited.

Monday, July 20 – Evening

I think I'm going to like this woman. She is kind. And direct. Her eyes are clear light, light blue. Like clear water. You can't tell whether it's shallow or bottomless.

I arrived early, unusual for me. I don't drive to the north side very often. It took less time than I expected. Something must have been urging me toward this meeting.

On the way some lines from the poem I wrote last week were swelling in my throat. Maybe they were pushing me.

> *Invisible sea serpent crawls underneath*
> *and sucks the light from the morning sky,*
> *siphons the color from my plants and food*
> *and drains the marrow from my words.*

For the last weeks, ages it seems, all the color has been sucked out of everything. I don't finish a thing. It's taken me all day to write a letter for the parish bulletin. I feel as if I'm stuck in matted underbrush, just pulling myself through the days. Maybe I'm dying inside. What if I really am? I certainly don't want to go on living. Not like this.

The door was open when I rang the bell. I waited a moment. I heard footsteps coming from the back. She held the outside screen for me. Friendly.

A warm vitality in her voice. "Marilyn, come in. I'm just having a cup of coffee. Would you like some?"

I was glad she didn't call me 'Sister.' I hate the word. I feel as though I'm being put back into the habit, the knot from the strings pressing into the back of my head.

I immediately liked her house, big and lived-in. A little garden of plants at the east window. From where I sat, I could read titles of books. Neumann, Woolf, Caldwell, Jung, of course. Little heaps of them. More near her desk in the next room, her office, it looked like. I was just thinking her office looked small when she returned.

She is a well-built woman, earthy and refined at the same time. Her hair looked wild, streaked gray, brushed off her face, whenever it was last brushed. She must have been washing dishes. I could smell the lotion she was rubbing on her hands. I was relieved when she sat down instead of inviting me into the next room. I didn't want to be in her small office.

Do I need to write all this? I have to. I want to be able to reflect on it all. I think this is going to be the most intense process I have ever been in, and I need to keep every note.

I began by telling her how flat everything seems. How dull, dead I feel. I'm just not myself.

She was listening so deeply, I felt as though my throat were coming untied. Things poured out I never expected to say. "I've let other people tell me what to do. I've given away so much of my life."

"Your life? Your life is the most important thing you have." There was a circle of concern around her mouth. "Who have you given it away to?"

She must have seen me close my door inside. I wasn't ready to tell her all that. I guess I was afraid of what she might think. Maybe I am living subtly what I think people expect of a Sister, even when I hate being put in the mold.

To whom *have* I given my life? I must begin to put down my own roots. It is time. I'm 41. Even writing that feels good.

I must work with this question. Not tonight, though. Tomorrow, in the morning. Or at least before our next meeting. I'm glad we decided on Mondays. That will give me the weekend to reflect, find out where I am.

Tuesday, July 21

My dream last night is urging me to get started:

I am moving from group to group facilitating a discussion. How many of these I've done. But this time I am carrying a six-month-old baby girl in my left arm. I am holding her carefully, very close. She has a chest deformity and a gaping hole for a mouth. I hear her wet breathing. Every now and then the phlegm gurgles in her throat, so I excuse myself from the group, go over near a tree, hold her upside down to let the mucus flow out on the grass. Nobody seems to mind. When I come back and sit with her, warm and close to my chest, I feel such a love for her. Exquisite. A radiant spirit inside her that is very beautiful.

I need to start getting some mucus out of my throat, stop closing my inside door.

To whom have I given away so much of my life? I thought I was giving it to God. I thought becoming a Sister would be something really special to do with my life. Everybody else seemed so ecstatic that reception day. A part of me did, too. But down inside, I felt the bishop's sermon was contrived, pat, unctuous. I thought there must be something wrong with me. Even the next day, when the two second-year novices were shaving our heads, I thought it an outrage. Others thought it hilarious. How much like teen-age boys we looked. I went into the bathroom and tried not to gag. I cried as quietly as I could.

I don't know where I am with God right now. God seems like a swirling fog somewhere behind me. Now and then there is a little patch of sun, but most of the time I don't turn to look. I just go on to the next thing that has to be done.

Our instructors in the novitiate talked a lot about God and about love, but I don't think we loved. I did all the right things. At times I felt alive: the challenge of a test or giving a presentation in class; or the special feeling of a feast day, the festive chant, the elaborate meal, and a 'safe' movie. But, generally, getting through a routine was all that mattered. There was a gray sea of boredom floating underneath everything I did.

Somewhere there was a mark on me, a call. I was a Sister, different from other human beings who married.

Though I certainly didn't want my mother's life. And I never thought I would be a Teresa of Avila. But I did love quiet and hoped someday I would find God. Still there was little time for quiet.

Everything was filtered through the Sister screen, what was right and proper for a Sister. I began to feel less, see less, although I wasn't aware of it at the time. I wouldn't let myself be critical or angry. I fitted in, convincing myself that whatever happened was right. I was happy enough with some friendships, some achievements, a little recognition. But there was something unreal, artificial about living that way. The silent gray sea slept down underneath. I don't think that was true for everybody, but it certainly was for me.

I wish I knew more about me . . . and I am afraid to know it. What would make me feel alive? Worthwhile? Enthusiastic about living?

I have never told anyone about an experience I had one summer night. It just couldn't be said. We were staying at Grandma's during Dad's vacation. Her house was small, so Jeanne, Jim, Andy, and I were each in our sleeping bags on the living room floor. Max, Gram's dog, was stretched out next to me. I remember waking up. I was half-asleep, looking at the stars. A sound like a thousand-voiced choir began to murmur and swell. My breath wouldn't move. The tears came down my face. I was inside the vibrating Sound, most loving, rocking me. And I was lifted up. Out. I was as large as the sky. A warm, strong voice rose. It seemed to be coming from inside me: "I am the One you are to know."

I could have stayed in that Sound forever. There have been long stretches of time when I have forgotten about the experience. But I know it is the feeling of this Sound that I have been waiting for, hoping for, all these years, that feeling of warm rapture.

How will I ever sort through all of this? And then what? This searching seems hopeless.

Monday, July 27

Iris has eyes only for people. Other things don't seem to matter. I wonder if she ever sees the dust on the rungs of the chairs. I doubt it. But I saw her notice the crack in my lip today. Old cold sores keep splitting open. She seems to be constantly aware.

I told her about the God I thought I had given my life to. Not about the Sound. I wasn't ready to share that with her.

I told her that the God who had meant so much to me — to whom I had spoken the words of the Psalms every day for years, the God Jesus said he loved — had disappeared. Had I been fooling myself all along? I've been reading a lot about the Goddess, but that image feels foreign, doesn't fit into my prayer yet. And now God is being written about as Universal Energy. Why bother if God isn't even a person?

Iris didn't say what she believed about God. I wonder what she does believe. She just looked at me, not judging, as though everything I said was all right.

I have been thinking about Iris a lot. I wonder about her relationship with her husband. She is so present and attentive all the time. I wonder whether he finds it challenging to be with her.

I envy her. She seems so focused and vital. When I left her today, I felt alive during the drive back. Things seemed more real. I don't know why. Tonight I feel darker than ever inside.

I just felt my breath shudder like a collapsing accordion, with the same off-key sound.

Sunday, August 2

Perhaps I shouldn't have said anything, but I trust my friend Bert. And I needed to talk to someone. The lake was calm, the light skipped on the water, almost mocking me. So I just started. "I'm having trouble letting my scissors lie on my desk. It was weird the first time it happened."

Bert's eyes widened as she turned to look at me.

I told her how I was sitting at my desk, cutting, chopping the notes from the talk I had thought I was going to give into crazy little pieces. How I had a hard time breathing around the feeling of an elbow digging into my chest, pushing me back.

Once more I had let myself be used. Richard had asked me for my ideas, so, of course, I had shared them. He had used my entire outline and given my presentation to the adult ed group without even a thank-you. When everyone had left after coffee, telling 'Father' how wonderful his talk was, he couldn't bring himself to say 'good-night' or even look at me.

I could see the anger rising in Bert. I hesitated a moment. "As I sat later, looking at my scissors, I kept staring at the points. They seemed to come alive, like a magnet."

"Why don't you get out of that parish?"

"I can't. I've only been there a little over a year, and you know how a change right now would look on my resume."

"But if you're so angry all the time that you want to attack everything with your scissors, it's time to do something."

I could see Bert was frightened. "I see Iris tomorrow. Maybe she can help me sort this out."

"Why bother seeing her if you don't talk about this?"

It was time to leave. We picked up our things and walked back to our cars. Bert and her living group were going out to dinner, their regular Sunday night. Her hug was tight. I felt her fear and concern.

Tell Iris? I wonder whether she will think I'm suicidal. I couldn't even bring myself to tell Bert all that had really happened.

I'm still puzzled and frightened by what *did* happen. Just after I started jabbing wildly into the notes, I felt two strong hands at the back of my head pulling me. They were like black velvet. The hands made a tunnel sucking me across the room and down. I thought I was dying. As I went down, my body rolled, head first, backward, further and further. Total dark at the bottom. I could see all these scissor points, all sizes, gleaming, weaving toward me and away in a giddy dance. I was riveted. What if I lost control?

What if Iris thinks I should be hospitalized? The provincials would have to know, and then the whole community would find out. God, no.

Tuesday, August 4 – Morning I was too exhausted to write when I came home last night. So much happened with Iris. I need to get all of it down this morning so I can really feel into it, know for myself what is happening, before I go back today.

I started out by telling Iris I wasn't sure I should have come. That I didn't know whether there was anything for me to talk about. At least that I *wanted* to talk about.

Iris must have sensed I was having a hard time. "Marilyn, take a long, deep breath."

Her words took me by surprise. I wasn't sure what she meant.

She stood up. "Like this." She drew in the air, expanded her abdomen, and then let out a slow, long breath. "This will help you feel better. I want you to do it. Breathing this way into your abdomen will make it easier for you to connect with how you really feel."

I felt awkward as I stood up. The whole thing felt strange. I kept pulling my shoulders up. Iris suggested I let my back broaden instead.

"Put your hands on your abdomen and feel it move out as you inhale, like I'm doing."

I couldn't believe how much her body moved when she breathed. I could see her breath move in a wave from her abdomen to her chest. And she didn't seem to care at all how she looked. She seemed so wholesome and free. I was finding it difficult. My hands felt stiff, frozen. I have such a hard time letting go. I'm always so conscious of how I look.

"Here." She took my hand. "Feel the breath fill my abdomen and then move all the way into the upper chest."

I could feel her muscles stretch and recede. Her abdomen was warm. I tried putting my hands on my body again. My breathing seemed shallow, and my hands were still cold. I felt uncomfortable putting my hands on my abdomen in front of her.

"This is your body, Marilyn. You have every right to feel it."

I began again. Several long breaths. Iris was right. I started to feel different. Something was changing in me.

I felt lightheaded. I had to sit down. I began to shake. The scissors were right there in front of me.

"What is it, Marilyn? It's all right to say everything here."

It all rushed out. I told her I kept seeing scissors coming at me. Sharp. Their points taunting me. They wouldn't let me alone. They kept coming at me. If I let them, they would just take over.

I wound my fingers around my thumbs to steady my hands. "I have to keep my scissors out of sight. In my desk drawer. Or everything starts to go black around me."

I could see her concern.

I told her about Richard taking my notes and using them. How I felt used, walked over like a piece of old carpet. "With the parishioners there, I couldn't say a thing." Even if they hadn't been there, I couldn't have said a thing.

"Every image that comes to us is our friend."

I never thought of these scissors as friends. I told Iris I was afraid she'd think me suicidal when she heard about the scissors. I guess I was really afraid I was becoming suicidal.

She looked at me. I felt the room expand. Open. Space.

"Suicidal. Do you want to stop living?"

From a deep place in me, the words rushed out: "No. No, I don't want to. I just can't go on living the way I have been. In fact, I won't." I touched some place in me I didn't know was there.

Iris urged me to come back again this morning and to bring my scissors with me. I have wrapped them in a heavy brown envelope and put them into my purse. I have to find out how to make these a friend.

Tuesday, August 4 – Evening

Iris asked me to hold the scissors in my hand. In the sunlight in her living room, and with her present, I didn't feel any of the terror I had the night I had sat at my desk.

I felt more calm, too, from the special breathing we did. I was more aware of how I felt. Deep breathing is a bridge to quiet and a feeling of more space inside.

I began to feel more comfortable as I held the scissors. They looked like the steel they are.

"Go back to how you felt the night you were using them with your notes. How did you feel?"

How did I feel? Even as I recalled the experience, my

chest became very tight. And my shoulders. I had been in a vice all that evening. As I thought about it again, a large knot got tighter and tighter in my throat. I could feel the wad beginning to choke me. I wanted to scream and I couldn't.

And there it was: A cat like the one at Uncle Art's farm that scratched me. That cat was in front of me. Only now someone had knotted its legs to its body and tied its mouth shut. It was all bound up with old rag strips. Its eyes kept looking at me as if I were responsible.

"It's a cat. I think it's dying. It's giving up struggling."

"Do you want to help it?"

"Yes, but how?"

She looked at the scissors.

I felt foolish, but I was determined to try. I worked with the scissors as if I were holding the cat, cutting and cutting through the rags and knots. I stopped.

"You mean I could cut through everything that's keeping me knotted up?"

"Yesterday you said you wanted to live. You can't live all knotted up."

"Do you really think I could cut through all the rags and knots that are binding me up like a corpse? Stand up and tell someone like Richard how I really feel, regardless of who else is or isn't there? I don't think I'm ready to do that yet."

Iris believes I will be.

I'm writing this tonight with my scissors in front of me. They look like plain ordinary scissors now.

What would happen if I ever started to cut free, *really* cut free? Where would I start to let go? My work? My parish? Saying what I really think? The community? All the dead clutter? My fear of what other people think? Where would I start or end?

Wednesday, August 5 A note from Bert. She is still worried. I haven't told her yet how much has changed after being with Iris.

It must have taken Bert hours to do the beautiful calligraphy. It flows like music on her card:

If you bring forth what is within you,
what you bring forth will save you.
If you do not bring forth what is within you,
what you do not bring forth will destroy you.

The lines were adapted from the Gospel of Thomas. Did someone else make up these words or did Jesus really say them? I hope he did. I need to keep remembering them.

Bert. So like her. I treasure her friendship. It's good to think about her. We started to become friends when we were both teaching in junior high. We went to classes together on Saturdays. She was finishing her masters in European history, and I was starting one in music.

Bert is a few years older than I am, but I always feel older. I had felt older the night she had stood at my bed and wakened me. I was younger, so I was sleeping in the small dorm with three others. She had a private room with a window only an arm's length from the neighbor's house with a small walkway between. She'd awakened to the sound of someone walking and had seen a man's head go past her open window. She had panicked. I went to look but saw no one. When I returned, I urged her to stay. We lay in bed,. and I held her until the quivering stopped and her breath pattern told me she was sleeping. It had been a risk. Any one of the others could have reported us for sleeping together, but something in me didn't care. I've certainly changed since then.

Bert and I could talk with each other, knowing what

we said would never be repeated. And that is something. I found I could talk with her about things I couldn't share with anyone else.

Our friendship had started my first year of teaching, the time I was trying to hold my own with Mary Andrew. Older, she loved to have a bevy of young teachers, especially bright ones, in her upstream current. She would enter the community room like a great ship, a galleon blown by a high wind. Especially that first year when we still had the habit, she sailed in with all the yardage of the old habit billowing and flapping. She sailed into my life suggesting I read the great Russian novels. Slavic music, Bergman films, current events — she had taken all in great sweeps and had been determined to give me a liberal education.

Disagreeing with Mary Andrew was not easy. She was very intelligent and had absorbed information from history, philosophy, literature — and she remembered. Challenged, she would jut out her large jaw, head shaking, finger pointing every word of her rapid flow. Sometimes when she had some wine, she would get flushed, invariably stir up a discussion that went to an argument. When her illogic caught up with her, she would churn the waters and, still shaking in defiance, would steam out.

She shook me, but I instinctively knew I had to hold to my own course. Without Bert, the galleon could simply have swept me under. Bert helped me through that first fall and winter. In her, I learned what 'friend' really means.

Friday, August 7

I was trying to breathe into my abdomen this morning, the way Iris showed me. Even with the bathroom door shut, I couldn't look into the mirror very long. I repeated her words: "This is your body, Marilyn." This is my body. I started getting anxious, a little faint.

It was the same feeling I remember having at a retreat when I had decided to confess all those sins for the final time. As I waited in line at the confessional, I began to have a sinking feeling. But I was determined to go through with telling this priest, whom I didn't even know, about my night experiences. I had promised myself that never again would I have to confess that I masturbated and received Communion the next morning without first going to Confession, that I had falsely convinced myself that I had stopped 'soon enough' or that I hadn't been fully awake. I had decided I would never again let myself start to feel even the beginnings of pleasure.

This morning, looking in the bathroom mirror, I was nearing those same feelings. I felt I was doing something wrong. But what is wrong with breathing and feeling my body become warm? My eyes looked more alive. But I know enjoying my body surely doesn't fit the Sister image. I realize as I write now I couldn't face the image of that cat all tied up again, that knotted-up cat that flashed in front of me when we worked with the scissors. Maybe I just couldn't stand the agitation. I stopped looking in the mirror and quickly opened the bathroom door.

When I came home from choir rehearsal tonight, I lay on the sofa. I was so tired. I knew what 'dead tired' meant. I felt that if I were just to lie still and totally let go, I would disintegrate, quietly die.

Maybe I simply don't have the energy to take hold and cut through all the 'rags,' the fears that are binding me.

Monday, August 10

I was telling Iris this morning I couldn't do the breathing in front of the mirror in the bathroom. Seeing myself naked felt wrong. "I know it's my body. I kept trying to say the words aloud to myself as you said them, but nothing helped. Something stops me."

"Stops you. What do you feel is stopping you?" She looked very directly at me. That's when I saw the ocean move in her eyes.

I hesitated. "I'm afraid of my body."

"Afraid?"

"Afraid of how I might feel. Where it might lead me, especially in the bathroom. When I see my body naked, I always think there is something wrong with me, with my body." My mother's voice shot into the back of my head. My whole body jerked.

"What is it?"

I swallowed and swallowed. The tears started to come. I tried to talk. It was so hard. "I just heard my mother's voice demanding that I stay out of my brothers' room. I can't believe something like this would come up now. I couldn't have been more than ten."

I had gone to the boys' bedroom to get my library book. My mother had seen me. She had gone for the flyswatter and hit and hit me with the handle. "You stay out of your brothers' room," she kept saying. She never even asked me what I had been doing there. The next day I had just gotten out of the tub and was looking at my body in the mirror. I was covered on my thighs and buttocks with blue and yellow-green welts. She came in to put some towels away. We just looked at each other. I had wanted her to see the bruises. All she repeated was, "Stay out of your brothers' room." I had wanted her to put the towel around me, hold me, and say she was sorry. She just walked out.

I started to cry, moan and cry all at once.

Iris reached over and gave me the shawl from the couch. I pulled it tight around my shoulders and cried until the sobs died out.

"It must be very difficult for you to remember your mother hitting you this way. Perhaps she herself had difficulty seeing her body, was afraid of her body. But you don't need to be afraid of yours."

The tea Iris brought was warm. We talked for more than an hour. Iris spoke with unusual intensity, conviction about the wonder of our bodies. "Exquisite, sensitive. The body is really the outermost feeler of the spirit. The body is spirit."

I know Iris said these words. My body is spirit. I'm reminded of Blake's, "The body is a portion of the soul." I have to spend time with this whole idea. Honoring my body feels radical. What is this consciousness, this wisdom in my body Iris says I need? She insists that if I am going to experience life fully, I have to get to know my body, really live in my body. I am going to have to take responsibility to develop my own vitality.

I'm whirling right now. Even my writing looks out of control. I can feel the tension in the back of my neck. Could I have been misled about my body all my life? Could my mother have been wrong? The Church? All those instructions I sat through, wrong?

My body, this body, is really not dangerous? Is really holy? In itself? I wonder whether it is really true that I can experience, feel, really connect with God through my body. I remember how I certainly felt the Sound holding and rocking my body.

Wednesday, August 12 I went to the community meeting tonight. I thought it would be good to participate in a community gathering. Bert might be there, with Pat and Evelyn, her living group.

But I hated all the rules and constitution talk. I felt as if we were spooning dead ashes in a cup. Over and over we turned the pages of suggestions. Rome's corrections to our proposed revisions.

I saw Bert looking more and more bored, and then disgusted. Finally, she said in a very quiet voice, "I'm too tired to go around again on this. Why can't we just live our own lives?"

People couldn't let in relief at the thought of it. I could feel their fear. Right away, all the old reasons. Loss of our apostolic approval. Taxes. The older Sisters would be terrified.

Why are we so afraid? I have been thinking a lot about fear. Our lives are in a straitjacket of fear. Certainly mine is. I want to be honest about my fears. I let little fears dominate me. I fuss with my hair and my clothes because I'm afraid I won't look good enough. I'm afraid someone will pass the lounge door and see me eating a piece of cake. I quickly look busy if I'm just sitting at my desk when someone enters. I was afraid of even trying to *look* at my own body the other day. My whole life is a web of fears.

Tuesday, August 18

I just finished sitting in front of my bathroom mirror, really trying to see my body. Last week Iris suggested I draw my body. I had been startled. Drawing is an excellent way, she said, to slow down and really *see* my body, not just look at it. She suggested that I note whatever feeling or memories came up. What parts of my body felt warm or cold. What parts I usually lived in more consciously. What parts I liked.

Yesterday I showed Iris my first drawing. I feel so warmed and safe in her presence. I had drawn as she suggested, but I hadn't taken very much time with it. She helped me see how I had concentrated on my eyes. How, when I look only into my eyes, I don't have to see the rest of me. My drawing looked as if I had put a sheath over the rest of my body. All the lines were faint. I had not seen my breasts. There were some vague dead lines. My head told me that my breasts were there in that space, but I had not seen the veins and the nipples, the fine hairs around them. I had not really seen them.

When we talked about breasts, Iris said, "Don't just think about them. Feel, feel into them." As we talked, I remembered my mother telling me to be careful how I walked, not to push out my breasts. I must have been about 11. She was describing a young girl entering a church hall for a dance and quoted some man saying something about "leading with her baby tits."

I cried as I listened to Iris speak so beautifully about a woman's breast. I'm crying a lot these days. So much of my life crammed into being careful. Sometimes I think I'm wasting time, certainly money, just sitting, using up Iris' Kleenex.

At the moment, an experience I haven't recalled in years is back. I was in my classroom, my chorus room. The janitor, a man in his fifties, kept coming in to check the radiator. One day he was already there when I came in. He moved toward me, grinning, putting his hands on my breasts. I was shocked and frightened. I blurted out as I backed out of the room, "You ought to go, get married."

My breasts. Iris says they are a symbol of a woman's power to nourish another life from the milk she has generated within her own body. What I have been trying to do is feed others from my head, with my ideas. I have ignored my breasts, ignored nurturing from my heart.

I took time this morning to draw my breasts again. My breasts. They felt warm like a little baby's face or like bread dough. El Shaddai — "the breasts of God," the ancients used to say of the mountains. I wonder. Do I always have to think 'holy' to make something good? My breasts looked radiant, like light inside alabaster. The light seemed to be flowing and falling with my breathing. My breasts looked beautiful as they are. My drawing hasn't caught it yet, but as I put the drawing from yesterday and this one together, I am amazed at how much I didn't see the first time.

Saturday, August 22

I hesitate to write Mark's name here. Some people know we are friends. I've never told anyone, not even Bert, how I really feel about him or how intimate our friendship is. Just the feeling that what I write here is outside of me, and that someone could read this journal, makes me hesitate. What am I afraid of? There is nothing to hide. We have a beautiful relationship.

Interesting, I haven't mentioned Mark to Iris either. I did think of Mark when I cried so deeply with Iris. The only other time I had cried like that was when I had been with Mark after my contract hadn't been renewed because of all the crazy gossip that I was directing the pastor. I had cried and cried. Mark had been so good. He had held me until the crying stopped.

Mark called today. He's back from New Orleans and his summer teaching. He needs to rest and do some reading. He has some new ideas for his Christology course. That's one of the things I like about him: He is always creative. And I like it that he wants to go over his outlines in detail with me. He'll call back next week, and we can set a time.

I am grateful I know him. We liked each other from the very beginning. We met when I started to work for my degree in pastoral theology. I had to get out of teaching. I was 31 at the time — ten years ago. He must have been in his early 40s, a stimulating teacher. After I had finished his course, we had continued to meet once in a while for lunch. He thought I should pursue a doctorate. The provincials didn't think so.

I'm always excited looking forward to being with him. We have enjoyed sharing things we like: art museums, concerts, films. I have introduced him to artists I like: Rouault, Barlach, O'Keeffe, Mestrovic. We've found we are both enthusiastic about Merton's writings. Mark has shared his love of Eastern writers. We've read and talked about Lao Tsu, the Upanishads, Merton's *Asian Journal.* We each discovered Bede Griffiths' *The Marriage of East and West* at the same time. We could argue, too, but it was always positive, fun.

Some part of me has come alive, become whole, because I've felt I am special and lovable to him.

I used to smile when couples paired off during workshops and summer sessions at the university. Thirty-year-old teen-agers. I was too sophisticated to allow myself to appear so immature. Even though I knew it was important for people to come alive. I felt I needed to see my relationship with Mark as deeper, more spiritual. I think that is why I saw our relationship in the pattern of Clare of Assisi and Francis. It has always intrigued me that these two medieval Italians who had loved each other so deeply were still saints. The interpretation always given was that theirs was a spiritual friendship.

I wonder what that is.

Monday, August 24 Today I realized that Iris and I don't really just talk. We move into another kind of space. We feel our way around in a room I have not been in before. Whatever happens, happens. This approach is such a contrast to the way I usually carefully prepare for a meeting.

Today I suddenly found myself asking Iris how I could change the way I feel about my body.

"Nothing really changes until you love. We love ourselves alive." And then she looked at her hand. It is a beautifully shaped, strong, competent hand. She said to it, "I love you." When she moved her hand to the back of her neck, she said, "My hand lets me say 'I love you' to all parts of my body." She explained that we need to thank the parts of our body that have been working so long to help us, absorbing the stress or anxiety we feel.

Why do I always have to go through a moment of feeling embarrassed? I certainly wasn't trained to be tender or loving to my body. When I looked at my hand, more brittle than hers, I could feel my fingers begin to tingle. When I began to rub the knot in the back of my neck, I didn't feel love. I felt anger, an old anger. I was back ten years.

Iris noticed right away.

I was standing in front of that big desk in the principal's office. Ann James was pointing her stubby finger at one of the girl's illustrations for the concert program. "No, no. We can't have these costumes so revealing."

Iris encouraged me to say what I hadn't been able to say then.

I screamed out, "Damn you!" All I had held in came rushing out. "Damn you! You want everything safe and dead. The students think you're stupid. They pity me for having to check everything with you. Damn it."

I stopped to get my breath. I was shaking but felt lighter.

I asked Iris to explain what had happened. Thousands of these situations, she said, get stored in our bodies, and we need to free ourselves from all our swallowed anger. When I asked her how, she said, "Do just what you did now. Get the anger out whenever a memory returns."

I was astonished that this memory had returned when I started to massage the back of my neck. How many stale experiences must be stored in my body. It may be all that old stuff congealed in my body that makes me feel heavy, depressed. I believe Iris. When a memory returns, I need to release the anger I have held back.

Monday, August 31 Iris told me today that she would be on vacation for the next two weeks, so we wouldn't be meeting next Monday. Anyway, Monday is Labor Day.

I felt a little panic for a moment. A half a month. What if I fall back into the old dead feelings?

Iris offered me a thin little book. *Wisdoms* by Dorothy Maclean. She said she uses it all the time and suggested I try to hear the words *inside*, the way the author first experienced them, a surging up of a deep inner voice.

I'm curious. Dorothy Maclean, who are you? How did you connect with this voice you call Divina?

I looked at the first entry tonight.

> *Don't listen just to the sound of the birds, listen to the quality of Nature behind them. As you focus more attentively in the silence, a clear voice comes and you soar, for it is My voice.*

I decided to practice listening for this quality in the morning. *Wisdoms* describes the inner quality of the birds' song as clear, outgoing, immediate, happy. I haven't heard any quality so electric for a long time. My meditations have been so boring that I'm grateful when I don't have enough time in the morning for them. No clear voice has come to make me soar. I wonder. What if I really did listen? Would

I hear that magnificent Sound again? It seems far away, like an old dream.

Tuesday, September 8

I drove home to spend Labor Day with Mom and Dad yesterday. What a mistake. I become unreal when I'm in the house, their house.

My mother has everything in her life and in her house so right. She buys the right blouse for my sister. She steams her vegetables the right number of minutes. She says the right thing to the parish council.

Mom picks at the least thing that doesn't fit her 'right' world. She doesn't like women reading at the liturgy. She believes women don't belong at the altar. Little girls don't belong in a boy's room. I wonder. Maybe she doesn't really like other women. Maybe that's why she won't let go when I don't agree with her. She keeps pushing and pushing. She needs me to say she's right.

At one point yesterday, Dad caught my eye. I think he sensed I was about to explode. His way of living with Mom was written on his face: 'Don't say anything. It isn't worth arguing about.'

I need to talk with Iris about these feelings. In the past I wouldn't let myself feel them. They seemed so petty, too picky. They keep coming up, though. I really need to say out loud all the reactions I held back yesterday. They are giving me a tight knot at the back of my neck.

The sad thing is Mom is so good. I would like to love her, like to enjoy being with her. She does so many things for all of us. Knits afghans for each grandkid. A tin filled with her cookies for me to take back. I think she wants me to love her, but I can't help needing to get away from her.

I don't want to spend any more time going over this

trip. Maybe I don't want to let in how much like Mom I am. I'm just not as obvious about always being right.

So much of my life I have had to be right. No matter what the test or game or challenge was in grade school, I had to come in first, had to have everything right. I was always first, even without trying. Mom loved my successes, but at the same time something made her want to keep me in my place. I have a sense she was not first very often as a child. She was proud that her daughter was, but resented my successes at the same time. Maybe 'resent' is too strong. I'm not sure.

Sometimes I think I am gifted. At other times, I see myself as just a good average. Yes, I'm book-bright, and I'm good at the piano and with the flute. I used to be really good with the flute, but not great.

I'm not great. But down in me something really does want to live. Fully.

Sunday, September 13 I need to gather my thoughts to write to Mark. We had such a fine evening together. We shared our summer experiences. At times, there was so much we wanted to say to each other, we laughed. We were both talking at once. He enjoyed New Orleans and all its ethnic color, the jazz and the flowers, not the humidity. I told him about seeing Iris.

Mark stopped eating. "Are you going to be all right?"

"I hope so. Sometimes I feel that I'm coming apart at the seams, but I do trust this woman."

Mark's card came yesterday in his special precise script, thanking me for the evening, the food, the music, 'nourishment for every dimension.'

He chose the Georgia O'Keeffe card of the brilliant red poppy. So much energy and life in it. So absolutely open, offering its color and rich black heart-center for all to see. That flower-moment of full being, just before the first outside petal begins to turn down, its life energy beginning to recede. No embarrassment, no arrogance. It is just exultant in its being, filling all the space and flowing beyond.

To say thank you to Mark for all he means in my life seems so faint and lame. I wonder what it would feel like to write freely of how much I love him, allow myself to be like this brilliant red poppy. I sense Mark would probably tear up the card so no one could read it, should something happen to him.

I would probably destroy the card, too — part of always being careful. A voice jumps in immediately with, "But what will people say?" I feel a constant crowd of people always following and watching. I give them such power. Who are all these people? I know from the pain in my stomach, from the fear of being judged wrong or inadequate, that they are very real. On second thought, they have helped me, too. Kept me from making a fool of myself at times.

Monday, September 14

I felt good being with Iris again this morning. She looked fresh, rested. I told her I had been spending time with *Wisdoms* in the mornings. Some of the passages didn't speak to me, but at least it had been something to turn to while she had been away.

I shared some of my insights about myself from my time with Mom and Dad. How annoyed I was at my mother's need always to be right. And how much I disliked the way she kept insisting I agree with her. How my dad just lets her have her way; most of the time he just goes quiet. I don't think he wants an argument.

I told Iris that, as I was journaling, it struck me how

much like my mother I am, only less obvious. I have needed to be right so much of my life. Even in an argument, it is important for me to be right in the end.

When I think about changing this pattern in me, I told Iris, I get confused. I remember the struggle I had in the novitiate. Marie Bernarde had been determined to make me humble and obedient. I can still see her slender fingers with her perfect nails resting on the pad on her desk. The perfect novice mistress. She was going to make sure I learned to speak with greater humility, which, to me, meant saying she was right when we couldn't agree. Often she would correct me for something ridiculously small. I tried to be submissive and surrender, but I never could accept, really apologize for what didn't make sense. It felt like a game to make me humble. I simply kept all my feelings locked inside.

"I don't want to be arrogant, always right, and I can't afford to be submissive if that means it's right for someone like Richard to use my outline, to walk all over me."

Iris assured me it is unhealthy to deny what I see. That is very different from needing to be right all the time. It would be good to find out what is underneath that need in me. Then she said something that surprised me. "It sounds to me as if you are also doing what your dad has been doing, keeping quiet to avoid an argument."

It's true. Like him, I swallow, knot all these wads in my throat. I became submissive like my dad in front of Marie Bernarde. That night with Richard in front of the parishioners, I said nothing. No wonder the cat and the scissors showed up.

Iris invited me to spend time to find out what is underneath this pattern in me.

She gave me a warm hug at the door. I could feel the soft bulges just above her waist.

I have been with the question most of the day, while

I was driving and during the in-betweens at work. What is it that prompts my mother's pattern of needing to be right and my dad's pattern of keeping still? I believe underneath both of my parents' patterns is fear. I sense that my mother fears she will seem inadequate. I know that fear in me. I touch into fear, too, around Dad, his fear that things will be unpleasant, or worse, there will be an angry scene. I think in the novitiate I was afraid if I opened my mouth and said what I thought, I would be sent home. At the parish I'm afraid I'd be told to resign.

Fear. What do I do with this fear?

Sunday, September 20

As I drove home last night, the clouds looked like long black whales with red underbellies. Twilight usually brings sadness, I told myself. Away from home as a kid, I always became homesick, really sick, about the time of twilight. But last night was different. The tears were gathering and starting down my face as the images of the women I had just left passed like a stream in front of me.

I had just finished a workshop on music and the liturgy. My strong point is helping groups meditate together into the present-day significance of the readings for the liturgy instead of hurrying to talk about appropriate hymns. Twenty-some community women from the area had gathered. What was hitting me as I drove home was how some of them were such large, powerful women, in charge, military. And in between were little bird-like figures, fearful and fragile, afraid they weren't getting it right. They all looked unloved and unloving. Several young women. Two I'm sure have a special connection. They at least looked alive and hopeful.

Something in me is overreacting, I'm sure. I sensed a lot of fear and unhappiness in those women last night.

Maybe I'm projecting my dissatisfaction with myself, with my life onto them. I am such sweet, soured custard. Why don't I make a clean decision and leave this community? I toy with the thought every now and then.

I tried to leave before final vows. Right now, all I can see of that morning sitting in Mother Gerarda's office is her placid face, and all I can hear is that oily voice: "This is a life of crucifixion, of striving for perfection for the love of God."

I thought I was going to vomit right on her desk, freshly polished by one of her secretaries. Rolls and rolls of old rags pouring out of my gagging throat, over her desk and over her, filling the room and winding out the windows to the street below.

Monday, September 21 Every time I get near sick spirituality talk, I get so frustrated. I stayed in community, I told Iris, because I wasn't sure that leaving was the right thing for me to do. I'm still not sure. Maybe if I just tried harder, I would find God or God would find me.

Iris said, "The main choice at the moment is that you decide to be true to yourself. That is more important right now than any other decision. Forget all the rest."

Forget? Tonight I can't seem to forget. Thoughts about making the decision to leave keep returning. Why not do it? Leave. Get the whole thing over with. But I feel the bottom half of me floats away at the thought of meeting with the provincial, sweet Elizabeth. She would probably not meet with me alone. She would have Diane with her, a steely reminder of the money questions, of justice to the community. I can already see Diane working her little gold pencil.

The old fear is rushing in. I know I'm not ready to make any genuine decision.

Monday, September 28 I am exhausted tonight. The only thing that comes to mind at the moment is the beautiful teal green sweater Iris was wearing today. I was so worked up when I got there, late for the appointment, that I didn't even notice the sweater at first.

Ellen had stopped me as I was leaving my office. She had apparently been meeting with Ralph, 'Monsignor,' as she needs to call him. Ellen had such gray-blue circles under her eyes. "Are you busy? I need to talk to someone or go crazy."

We sat down. I watched her swallow, finally, "Ray and I have been drifting apart." And then in a rush to get it all said, she told me she hates going to all her husband's coaching events. He gets bored with her music. He resents it when she accompanies Lois or James for their concerts.

Her voice picked up a new angry, defensive tone. "He keeps letting me know that my interests aren't in the real world." She looked away, her chin quivered. "James and I enjoy our rehearsals. Enjoy each other. We both wish we were free to be married."

"Have you talked about this with Ray?"

"No, I can't. We had intercourse last night. Ray said we had 'a good lay.' I felt empty. That's how little he really knows me. I think we should separate before I start hating him. My asthma is getting worse. Most of the time I feel dead."

I felt I was on a high swing, unable to stop or get my balance. Ellen and I were in the same empty space, just different settings. We were both trying to fit into something we promised and were both feeling trapped.

"Monsignor said I should pray about it. Perhaps come to Mass more often. He told me I would find the strength I need to be a good wife."

What rot. Where did this priest ever find out what a good wife is? And why does he think everything gets solved by quoting Scripture? I resent more every day what this Church is doing to women.

I really couldn't do much to help Ellen. I wish I were in a better place myself, a place where I could help her. More like Iris, who would know what to do.

Tuesday, September 29 I want to remember something else from yesterday's meeting with Iris. We sat for a long time — at least it seemed long to me — just breathing. I'm usually too self-conscious to look steadily into someone's eyes. 'Locking eyes,' we used to say as kids. But with Iris, my breathing started to match her rhythm, slow and long. We didn't talk, but I began to feel relaxed. That's when I first noticed her sweater.

I need to breathe this way more often. Iris suggested I use my mirror, look into my own eyes, breathe with myself. I can't seem to do this alone, not for very long. My thoughts keep pulling me away.

Wednesday, September 30 Adrienne Rich's introduction to *The Other Voice* caught hold of me far down inside: "Finding our voices." The married Ellens haven't found their voices. Of course, my dad doesn't use his either. And those of us in community certainly haven't found ours. What has been written or spoken even among ourselves that is true to the marrow of us? We epitomize the silencing of women. The Three Marias in *Letters from the Portuguese* say all women have been cloistered, removed from public life and decisions, servants to faceless institutions, praised for their submission.

When I think of all those retreat sessions with the retreat master and his demeaning stories about women in community, and all of us sitting obediently silent, I get such a headache.

Once at a retreat I had written in my notebook, "We are being herded into our places like cattle to their stalls." I must have left the book in the dining room. I was summoned to Mother Gerarda's office. She was horrified and explained that a good Sister would never think such thoughts. What she was really saying was that a good Sister never thinks and has no privacy. How could we expect to find our voices when we weren't even supposed to think and feel?

It was the five of us meeting on the back stairs in the semi-dark who began to talk and to find our voices. The terrazzo was cold to sit on, but we didn't mind. We talked and argued and laughed. It was risky and exciting. We felt alive. I know much of the vitality and changes in the school came from those meetings. We supported each other.

Monday, October 5

I have been tearing up and throwing away old snapshots whenever I find them. My sister, Jeanne, put an old photo of me in the card she sent for my birthday. One of those school pictures of me in second grade. Mom's writing is on the back.

When I look at this little girl, a dream I had last summer washes up in me. It had awakened me one night about a week before I started to see Iris.

> *I am in a large dark basement. Sick, dying horses are lying in stalls. They are all infected. Old puss is gathered around their eyes and nostrils. I see the rheumy eyes of a black one. It lifts its head as I come toward it. I have a little girl about three years old by the hand. I run with her angrily up and down the aisles. I have to get her out before she becomes ill. I run with her up the stairway screaming, "Somebody call the health department." I scream myself awake.*

I feel I need to apologize to this little girl in the picture. She was so herself. How she loved her long string of clear-glass beads with the six square red ones. How she delighted in them. And the red satin bow in her thick black hair. Where did this young girl go?

I can remember her thrill at reading stories about birds, the ecstasy of losing herself in the bird world, spending hours with Mother Wren, washing her tiny bird dishes and hanging her stamp-sized dish towel on a twig outside the bird house.

That same summer she would lie near a weed bluebell in the park, thinking if she could get still enough and near enough she could hear it ringing.

I had many good moments as a child. But often I carried an adult weight. It seems I was always worrying about my brothers, Andy or Jim — mostly Jim — getting into trouble. I can still feel the ache of seeing the hole in the heel of my sister's stocking and how she was trying not to have it show. I kept vigil to see whether or not my mother and father were in a good space with each other. In some ways, there never was a child within.

I showed this photo to Iris this morning. Her reflections disturbed me. She saw a little girl who was already conditioned to make sure she would be pretty. We talked about her smile and the tilt of her head. She was pleading to be liked.

Iris asked me to try to feel into the *un*conditioned child, the one I was before I learned what I had to do to be accepted. "*Wisdoms* speaks of our original design, our original basic pattern." She picked up her copy from the coffee table, turned some pages, looked at me, and began to read:

> *The pattern for each one of you is very alive within, trying to express itself and waiting for you to cooperate with it. You say you lose your individuality when you give up choice. No, you find it. You have a basic pattern which is perfect. I can tell you the perfect step to make each moment.*

I hate that passage, I told her.

She smiled, half-surprised and half-questioning. Then her voice shifted: "Something inside you is hurting?"

"Confused. I'm trying to get out of this 'God's will' talk. That passage reminds me of the emphasis in high school about having a special call, a vocation. The promise that if we followed God's will, we would become women of deep spirituality. I think I've been on the wrong road or at least going the wrong direction on the spirituality road. I hate talk about vocations."

Iris referred to the passage again. "The original pattern of who you are, who each person is, is not about having a special vocation, not at all."

I've been reading the page again. I keep fighting with every sentence.

There must be something I'm not getting. It's just too passive, too sweetly submissive. I need to let this book go for now.

Saturday, October 10 My birthday. I was shocked at the gray hairs showing up after I washed my hair this morning. If my hair weren't so dark, the gray probably wouldn't show so much. The last time Jim and his family came, I was surprised to see all the gray at his temples. Younger brothers shouldn't get gray so soon.

Why do I fear aging? I have a feeling my life is running out and I haven't really lived, really taken hold and decided how I want to live. I don't have a sense of what my basic pattern is.

I am getting older. I can feel it in the way people look at me. It meant so much to me to be the youngest faculty member. There was always a group of students around me, laughing and teasing. And listening. I wonder what I would feel like now if I were on the faculty as one of the middle-aged group.

Be honest. Being liked meant a lot. Having students confide their resentments and dislikes, their pregnancy fears, gave me a sense of significance. My height and white skin and black eyebrows were assets then.

Now all that seems flat, immature.

Sunday, October 11 — Morning The light was different in the room this morning. It seemed clearer. When I walked into my living room, I saw the brilliant red of Mark's plant. The sun was hitting it full face.

Yesterday when I took off the florist's paper and saw the abundance of blossoms, I was in the park again on the walk Mark and I had taken early last summer. All along the gloxinias. Here was the same pulsing red, not bright, more purple red, warm and deep. How sensitive of Mark.

I looked in the file for the poem I had written when I first sensed his depth. I had been listening to a flute recording of "The Heart of the Inca King" when the inspiration for the poem came. It was the first of my 'Clare to Francis' poems.

When I wrote the poem, I imagined what might have happened inside Clare as she stood at the central fountain in Assisi on a summer night in 1210 and heard Francis speak for the first time.

Clare to Francis

The blood of God stirs and runs in your heart
never still; never disturbed.

Your god-blood tumbles down heart-mountains
far, serene, black purple
standing in a glass-blue night.
Your blood, warm shadows, spreads over the long,
level sand valley, moves over my body
seeking until it finds an open artery
and waterfalls into my heart.
An ocean beating, surging in one small cave.

The blood of God stirs and breathes in you
never still; never disturbed.

I think that was when I knew for certain that I loved Mark, and there was nothing I could do about it. Except how I expressed it.

And now, I'm concerned. We are becoming more and more intimate, physically intimate. We embrace a lot. It seems so right when we are together and so confusing inside later.

Sunday, October 11 – Evening

The sun was bright this morning, but the air was chilly, a first fall chill. The trees were in full color as we drove to the lake. Bert said nothing.

I was puzzled. This was supposed to be my birthday lunch. Bert had dark shadows under her eyes and thin new lines on her face. The pores in her skin are always bigger when she hasn't slept.

Then she told me. She let me feel the lump on her breast. It was hard like a cherry pit, larger.

Our lunch sat untouched on the seat between us as we looked out at the lake and the gray and green swathes playing over each other.

"I don't want surgery . . . and I'm afraid not to have it." Those smoky gray eyes of hers.

I wish I could have said something hopeful or something profound, but I couldn't. Everything that came to mind seemed so hollow. The thought of Bert with a swollen, massive left arm froze me. Not Bert. I locked fingers with hers. "Bert, you have to have a biopsy. How else will you know? I'll go with you."

Tonight as I put down my thoughts, I feel numb and angry. Why do so many of us, so many young women in community, have cancer? Something is terribly wrong. We say it, but we don't do a damn thing about it.

Monday, October 12 – Morning

I woke up in terror. A nightmare:

A rat is eating at my left breast. It chews off a bit, runs away and comes back, until my whole breast is gone. There is a gaping hole in the center of my chest. Only there is no blood.

Something inside me is eating me or eating at me.

Monday, October 12 – Evening

My time with Iris today was too short. I thought I'd be talking only about the nightmare, but things I've been carrying for years came pouring out. We were talking about Bert's lump and my anger and the dream. I dreaded picking up the dream.

Iris sees dreams the way Jung describes them, as letters from a friend in the night, alerting us to something we haven't been aware of.

"What is this rat telling you? What feels as if it were eating at your breast?"

Without thinking I blurted out, "My fear of sexual feelings."

I have lived with that fear for a long time. I felt a heavy sludge in my stomach as I began dredging it up.

It was during my first year in community. Saturday after lunch was the routine time for scrubbing the kitchen floor. We were each given an area to scrub. I could feel Marie's eyes on me from a distance. She had been slipping poems into my books, love verses, sentimental. At first, I thought they were her own. Then I saw her in the library copying them on the small loose-leaf sheets she used. I liked her, in a way. She was athletic, healthy-looking, quite sensitive.

I must have been asked to get some clean rags from the basement storeroom. I wasn't too surprised when Marie followed me down 'to help.'

I was hurrying to leave the basement room when she moved close to me, hugged me, and gently touched my breasts. It felt so wrong, frightening. I pulled away. "Marie, I have to go."

Several days later, as we were washing dishes, I noticed some red gauges on her hand, between her thumb and first finger. I think now she must have been punishing herself for those feelings she couldn't control.

And then came that heavy pall of people being called

for questioning. Someone was being sent home. Marie, of course. I was never called. It was a relief. I was safe. What a coward I was. I never talked to her, never said good-bye. So typical of me. I was shaping a deep part of me always to be careful, always to be right.

Iris is the only one I'd ever told this experience to. When I finished, I looked at her. I know she saw the tears that stood in my eyes. It all seemed understandable to Iris.

"What frightened you the most with Marie?"

"That I would be caught doing something very wrong. Letting someone touch me. I have to be honest here and say it out loud. I know when Marie touched me so lovingly, I felt good. I began to feel excited. And afraid at the same time. Afraid and guilty. Guilt frightened me more than anything. It still does."

Iris waited for me to continue. I was on the swing again, out of control. Mark. I hesitated. Then plunged. "Well, with Mark, my friend, I let him take the lead. If it's right for him, it must be all right for me."

I realize as I write this, that is what I have been doing. I've been giving my responsibility to Mark, giving away my own responsibility.

"Mark and I are very good friends. We've known each other for ten years. We're close. We hug each other with delight when we meet. We kiss. Mostly we talk. It's wonderful to save things — experiences, ideas, special things, disappointments — until we are together. We like to sit close with our arms around each other. It's exciting, but we are always careful. We never let ourselves go too far. We respect each other's life choices."

"What effect does this have on you?"

"It's always a strain. I'm afraid of the pleasure. I know the power it can have over me when I begin to feel excited. I don't want to go down through all that guilt again."

"So you are always on guard, against feeling pleasure?"

As we talked, I began to see how I have been living all scrunched together, rigid, holding myself in a vice. No wonder the rat is chewing me. Iris believes we are meant to live fully, fully alive, vibrant and radiant.

My mind is churning tonight. How can it ever be all right for me with my vow to enjoy sexual feelings? Could there be something radically unhealthy about celibacy? How can I think this way? I can't look at this any more tonight. I feel as if I'm being sucked down again. It's almost midnight. I need to get to bed.

Monday, October 26

"Tell your friend, please, that I will be very mindful of her today."

Iris put so much love in the words. I called to tell her I had to cancel our meeting because I was taking Bert to the hospital and needed to stay with her. In a way, I was relieved. Even with the relief in telling Iris about Mark, I'm beginning to fear where our sessions are taking me. Where her question about pleasure is taking me . . .

The outpatient department was in a swirl of talking and nurses and carts and a constant run of calls over the sound system. The row of patients, stretched all along one side of the corridor. Nervously waiting, I could feel the pain and the anxiety. It was very deep in Bert, too, as we went to the desk to check in.

We had tried to breathe calmly in the car on the way. Things seemed quiet until we couldn't find a parking place. Then the old anxiety rushed in.

Family or friends — bored, impatient, some worried — came from the lounge to check on the patients.

Bert and I sat waiting for her to be called. I wondered how many of these people — some looking very weak —

were concerned about death. I wondered, too, how many of these trips we would be making if Bert needed radiation. In some old-fashioned way I was praying to God.

When I came back at four to pick Bert up, she was sitting on the side of the cot. "They don't have a report yet." Her voice was papery, just the way she looked. Pat and Evelyn had decided to come to take her home. So I left.

I put on Faure's *Requiem* and laid on the floor in my living room. The majestic bass vibrated through the carpet. I let the sound fill all my cells. The tears rolled down the sides of my face into my hair. Death. Enormous door after door opened letting a peaceful procession of the dead move on and on into the mystery. Death. Bert. If not now, someday. And Mark. The baritone solo pierced with its sweetness. Mark. How much of me will die with your death?

Saturday, October 30

I shared the poem I wrote on Monday with Mark as we drove into the countryside. He wanted to hear it again. I told him about the experience of listening to Faure's *Requiem* and how I later connected with Clare's fear of Francis' death when she learned of his illness.

Clare to Francis

On which side of your death will I walk?

The procession, measured, unswerving,
lost, lost
winding higher, relentless
over the bones of the mountain forehead.
No tree, no bird, no flower.
Great blunt boulders
impassive, blind

No one to hear the frozen cry.

Will the flow of your breath be fading,
that god-breath hollowing, opening,
playing its own echo.

What can I create with you
when I walk on this side of your death?

We got out of the car. The sky was overcast. A gray-yellow over everything. We walked quietly. The ears of corn were dropping down, and the stalks looked ragged. Mark is supple — he's easy to walk with; he jogs a lot. We stopped to watch the geese fly over. I wondered what it would be like to be married to him. I had forgotten how handsome he is. I noticed a little red cut on his jaw from shaving too close.

"Mark, why did you choose celibacy? Do you find it good for you?"

He turned, facing me. "It's part of the package. I wanted to teach, and I liked the guys in this community."

"Do you believe celibacy has value?"

He looked away, as if he were watching the crows. "I didn't want to take on my dad's drugstore. I wanted to do something special, and I liked the university world. I enjoy what I do." He stopped and looked at me. "I'm grateful for our friendship. I value it." He grinned. "I think I've just learned to live with it, but celibacy itself means less and less." He shrugged.

I sensed that Mark had been thinking about the whole question. But I don't think he was ready to talk about it. And I have to do some more thinking for myself.

Sunday, November 1

I am beginning to hate, I mean *really* hate, parish meetings. An entire evening every two weeks and little to show for it. And I am so mad at Richard. The liturgy this morning was old. And plodding. We were all being chloroformed.

I wonder where the title 'Father' for priests came from. Father Richard. At least ten years younger than I am . . . and so pompous. Father. Jesus was never called 'Father.' And neither were his followers, Peter, James, and John. I wonder when the title began. I know the practice should stop because it gives a false power aura around the priests.

Sometimes I see 'Father' Richard as a second-grader, sandy-haired, standing with one foot on top of the other. He could have been very lovable then, smart, quick, full of ideas. Rick. And now he is so stuffed. He lives inside all the regulations, seems to get life from always knowing what is right. Sometimes I wish he would get roaring drunk and make a total ass of himself.

I wish I could like him more so it would make sense to talk with him. I was hopeful when he was selected to work with the Liturgy and Life Committee. I thought he would bring some creative ideas. I think he sees his role as corrective, steering us along the careful path. The members just go silent in front of 'Father.'

Our meeting to plan for Advent was a disaster. So now we'll sit with the same old stuff. Advent wreath and all the trite ceremonies we had finally gotten rid of before he came.

Yes, I know. It isn't only the liturgy questions that are getting to me. It's all this stuff — celibacy, sexuality, community — all I'm putting on hold. I know I'm a walking volcano. There just isn't time. Time to read, time to think, time to meditate. Time to write my head clear. Time to live, really.

I know I'm taking too many Anacin. It's the only way I can keep the back of my head from exploding.

Monday, November 2

I wish I could be free the way Iris is to talk about my body and my feelings. She brought out two prints of Georgia O'Keeffe's. Iris knows how I like O'Keeffe's work. We sat looking at the prints. "Sweetpeas" and the famous "Black Iris." I read somewhere that O'Keeffe says there is no connection between her flowers and female genitals. But I could feel a shift inside myself as I imagined the connection. The prints are very beautiful.

Iris offered to let me take them home for my reflection. To her, they become a beautiful presentation of the vulva, labia, and clitoris.

"Radiant. Really the genitals of the flower."

I began looking at the prints tonight. Iris told me earlier this morning the more I accept the powers of my body as mine, the freer I will become, the more myself I will become. Everything, even this turmoil swirling in me, is urging me to own my life, to name who I am. She suggested returning to drawing as a way of appreciating, accepting my whole being. I did not know how difficult it would be to draw my genitals.

I wasn't sure I had the courage to do the drawing. I imagined Iris coming in to sit with me in front of my bathroom mirror. I wanted to make her presence as concrete as I could, inviting her to sit on the edge of the tub. I couldn't see her face clearly.

As I started to draw, I suddenly saw the face of my mother. Her mouth was twisted in utter disgust. A grown woman sitting on the bathroom floor in front of a full-length mirror with her legs apart.

What was I even thinking of? I could feel my stomach turn and start to heave. When I looked up, my mouth in the mirror looked exactly like my mother's. "This is awful, ugly, nasty." Her words were coming out of my mouth. Something is really wrong with this. It's repulsive.

My body was rebelling. I knew I was going to gag. I stood up, grabbed the drawing and, without looking, tore it to bits and flushed the pieces.

I went to bed, but I kept turning and turning. I got up and heated some milk and decided to write this down to get it out of me so I could go to sleep. It's almost 1:30.

Tuesday, November 3

I froze. I knew when I opened my eyes I would see the wall facing the bed covered with bleeding rabbits that had been thrown violently up there. Their bodies, mangled. Their genitals, crushed and hanging out of their bodies. Blood running down the wall. Bits of fur stuck in the blood. They weren't there . . . but they were.

I felt sick as I went toward the bathroom. I wanted to call Iris. I wouldn't let myself do that. But I think I am losing my mind. I feel as if I'm pounding my fists, screaming inside. Nobody can hear me. Maybe I am like those rabbits: my blood running out but I'm still not dead.

I have to get myself ready to play the organ today. The dirty crud on the keys left from Jay's sweaty fingers always disgusts me. God, I have to go. I can hear Iris saying, "Breathe and relax."

I don't have time. And it just doesn't work. Nothing works.

Wednesday, November 4

I didn't sleep in the night. I was afraid I would see those ghastly, bleeding rabbits again when I woke. When I picked up my purse and started for work, I was shaking all over. I couldn't stop it. I couldn't call Bert. Mark? I finally reached Iris.

She asked whether I thought I could drive. When I heard her voice, the shaking began to let up and I knew I could.

As soon as we sat down, I started to tell her about my mother's face in the bathroom, about the dream, the bloody wall. Her whole body listened.

"Let's see how this dream can help you."

I said I'd try. We had done this once before. I knew it would take me a little while to get into it.

"There's a part of you that feels like those helpless rabbits. Feel into them. Breathe very slowly. I'm going to ask you some questions. Just let the rabbits say whatever comes up. Give them your voice."

I closed my eyes and moved inside. Deep inside me where I felt the rabbits quivering. So was I.

"When you were well and playing around . . ."

"We never played around. We were in a pen."

"How did you feel?"

"We had food and water. But we never had a chance to run free, feel the grass. We never had our own real place in the earth."

"Who locked you up?"

"She did."

I looked up at Iris. "I did?"

"Stay with the rabbit feeling. Breathe slowly again and connect with the rabbits."

I found the rabbits again.

"Did you ever run free?"

"No. Nobody would let us out."

"How did you get thrown against the wall?"

"She did it. She was angry."

"Why was she angry?"

"She can't be free."

"So she threw you against the wall?"

"I didn't. I hate this. This is crazy. I hate this." I felt

wired. I started to scream. Stood up. A wild current tore through me. I threw my journal against the wall. "Damn it." My purse, my sweater, my car keys, the pillows. "Damn it." A plant toppled over. I didn't care. "You're pushing me. You are pushing me. I'm going crazy."

I was screaming and crying all at the same time. "I'm not some old goddamn bleeding rabbit." I collapsed on the floor.

Tonight, I wonder who I really am. I'm certainly not myself. I'm falling apart, out of control. The more I try, the worse it gets.

I don't think I can keep working and sorting through all this. I need time. Time. I know there is no way I can get open time now. Impossible.

Monday, November 9 I don't know how much longer I can hold everything together. I talked with Iris today about how much I wish I could have a long vacation. I'm not doing good work at the parish. I can't sleep. And I can't settle down long enough to come to grips with so much that's disturbing me.

Iris told me about a time in her life when she drove herself. Completing a dissertation, keeping her home together, teaching, not sleeping, battling a perpetual headache. How well I know that feeling. Finally she collapsed with massive pneumonia.

"I had to put everything on hold for a year. And that's when I learned to live."

Iris asked me whether I could give myself a year. "Time with no responsibility but yourself. Why should you have to get sick to have time?"

I could feel my whole body begin to brace against the possibility. How could I? "It's not possible. I could never let myself do that."

"You're not making the decision yet. Let the idea play through you."

It doesn't seem possible, and yet I ache for it, ache all over at the thought of it. Time with nothing to do, time with nothing hanging over me, time to start knowing what I really believe.

Tonight I want to look at every thought or fear or feeling I have about taking off a year.

If I were to let go of my work in the parish, what would happen? I worked hard for the increases, the health insurance, the car. What about the rent I need to pay? Interesting, my strongest concern is to hold on to this apartment. And if I left this work, what would I do in the future?

The people here like me, too. Ellen and people like her tell me I really make the parish, though I know I haven't been myself lately. Walk away? I can't abandon them. Perhaps I could work part-time. No. There would always be something out there to draw me into it. I would end up with a part-time breakdown.

The community? What would people say?

Bert? I know she would support me. Her group would agree.

The provincials? Maybe Iris could write a letter to them. No. That would be more handing over my responsibility. If I decide to do this, I would need to present this request myself. I think they'd be disturbed, wonder whether this meant I was planning to leave the community. They would very likely be concerned about my needing financial help. If I wasn't working, would they let me stay here? Such an ideal place. Mrs. Harris has been good to me, so easy to get along with. This apartment is really my first real home. I love the light and the trees in the park.

My family? They would worry. I'd tell them later, after

I was sure I was going to do this, when it was all set and under way.

Mark? I guess the real question from him would be whether or not I choose it. Do I really want to do it? And what would I plan to do with a whole year? He might think of it as a sabbatical. He would probably think I should go away to study, the great cure.

Jeanne, my responsible sister, couldn't have a year like this. Other women seem to be able to cope. Iris would say that I'm not 'other women,' and certainly they aren't living my life. Why should I have to prove I am as capable, as strong as I think other women are? Besides, how do I know what's really happening inside anyone else?

As I was leaving today, Iris said, "Keep listening to the deepest place in you that you can reach. And let yourself be guided."

Saturday, November 14

Bert is going to have the lump removed. She's thinking about having it done during Christmas vacation so she won't miss any teaching days.

When I told her I was thinking about taking off a year, she couldn't believe it. "Do you think it can happen?"

I told her I hadn't decided for sure yet.

I suggested she have the surgery now. The school wouldn't fall apart. There's a fund budgeted for substitutes. Bert's the one who needs the year off.

She shrugged her shoulders. She said she didn't want to disrupt things or baby herself. "Doctor Acher doesn't think there will be any complications."

How does he know?

"Bert, have it done now. And use the Christmas vacation to get your strength back."

We left the coffee shop. Bert still wasn't convinced. I realize how difficult it is for most of us to break free of expectations. We'll die before we let go of any of our work responsibilities.

When I feel the heavy pressure Bert is under, I know that is no way to live. I know, too, for me to continue living as I have been these past months is impossible. But it is easier to try to convince Bert to give herself time than it is to convince myself.

Friday, November 27 I feel relieved today that Thanksgiving and the trip home is over.

Dad's health is failing. I was stunned yesterday to see how watery and faded his eyes looked. He thinks his ulcer is, as he says, 'acting up again.' I think he is tired, tired of everything.

Now that I think of it, he never did look comfortable carving Mom's elaborate turkey. I know he didn't want to go through the charade yesterday. But Mom coaxed.

I feel, too, he is uncomfortable with his sons. Andy just leans back and studies his shoes or lets his kids crawl over him or comb his hair. He's so much like Dad. Jim talks too much trying to keep the party alive.

I think Dad could enjoy being with Jeanne and me, but Mom watches us all the time. A long time ago when I was about 12, Dad had said, "You are getting to be a nice looking young woman." Mother's eyebrows had gone up.

In a sense Dad has adjusted to a small world. His hours at the office are long. CPA work must get boring. He fits inside Mom's world at home. I think the only time he really lives is when Mom is still asleep and he sits at the kitchen table with his coffee, looking out the window at the 'weather.' It's his own little 'apartment.' I believe his private space and time is as important to him as mine is to me.

I can remember a few times in high school when I would get up early to come in and sit with him. Once he told me in his quiet morning voice, "You're too young to go to the convent. You need to try out more of life. Go after college if you want to." I think he resented Mom's pushing, telling everybody about my decision before I was even sure, but he never said so.

I'm glad I held to my determination not to stay overnight. I knew I was at the limit of what I could take. The snow/rain helped convince them I needed to get back. I didn't tell them I had decided to request a year off and needed to get ready for a meeting with the provincials. I'll tell them about it when I know for sure what is going to happen.

Saturday, November 28 I haven't done much of anything today. I was going to do some laundry and then decided to wait. I was going to clean the house, but I started paging through some old magazines. A mini tug-of-war went on inside me. I knew I should get to work, but I didn't feel like it. In the end I went into neutral and simply sat paging through issues of old magazines without really reading anything. Late this afternoon I stacked the sorted heaps back into the cabinet and looked for something to eat that I wouldn't have to cook.

The provincials have changed the meeting to a week from Thursday. Edith, their new secretary, called.

I want to invite Bert over for lunch tomorrow, but I haven't called. Perhaps I can make an omelet. Maybe she won't want to come. She's decided to wait until Christmas vacation to have the surgery, and she won't want to hear my protests.

Mark just called. He had a good relaxing time with his brother's family. And he wanted me to know he got his flight settled. He is going to spend his Christmas vacation and part of the semester break in New Orleans. He needs to meet with the dean about next summer. Some new friends have invited him to celebrate Christmas with them. I am pleased for him. He needs the time away. It will be warm in the South. But my voice didn't sound very spontaneous to me. I will miss our special Christmas time.

This headache. It's a pounding radiator.

Advent tomorrow. I used to look forward to it. It was a time of being in the night mystery, the dark, waiting. It was a time of touching inner depth. The readings for tomorrow, those ringing words from Mark's Gospel, "Awake. Be constantly on the watch," used to echo and echo inside. The swelling pathos of Handel's "Comfort Ye My People" would set an electric longing circling among all of us in church. Advent used to be warm and good and led me to a prayerful place far down inside.

Nothing of that feeling now. Even as I write these words, they seem flat, trite. I was hoping to revive some feeling with them. My inner ear has gone deaf.

I shouldn't play the organ tomorrow. It isn't fair to those who come hoping to begin a genuine Advent.

Thursday, December 10

The meeting with the provincials was complicated, careful, grotesque in a way. We never quite revealed our real fears and feelings that moved underneath. Very different from how I feel when I'm with Iris.

Diane, of course, was at Elizabeth's right. A shorthand

notebook on her corner of the desk. Rita sat at Elizabeth's left, at a little distance, as if an invisible chair were between.

I felt tense, sitting alone on the opposite side of the desk.

Everything came out too rehearsed. I explained how exhausted I am all the time, that I needed to get some distance from the parish. I haven't been doing justice to the work. Dr. Clayton has been helping me for the last few months to find a healthier way to live. I would continue to meet with her. All the while I was explaining, I was trying to balance on a point between being self-assured and needing permission.

I had the feeling that the three of them were moving back and forth between trying to be compassionate listeners and, at the same time, letting me know they were the decision-makers.

I felt relieved but unclean as I drove home. Relieved, because the meeting was over. Unclean, because I guarded the real truth about what is happening to me. I certainly wouldn't tell them about the bleeding rabbits on my wall.

I was only partially successful. They decided I should request a sick leave from the parish for six months, not for the year I had hoped. We would meet after six months to evaluate.

Six months to sort out this whole thing? But, by agreeing, at least I don't have to move from this apartment. Six months. Until the end of summer. What if I'm no better then? We'll see. It's a relief the meeting is over, and I don't have to make contact for six months.

I was just thinking how helpful it would be if each one of these women could work with Iris for a few months. They seem to be more provincial executives than genuine caring women. Perhaps they could be both, then.

Monday, December 14 I woke this morning just as the light was separating the trees from the sky. Out there, everything seemed peaceful. In here, and inside me, a whirling craziness, wild, angry. By the time I arrived for the meeting with Iris, I was about to explode.

"I'm afraid I can't hold on until January. Everything is getting to me. I'm angry at everything. I may really go crazy, start throwing things again and screaming."

"You can certainly do that here."

I told her that on Saturday, before I could talk to Ralph — Monsignor — Elizabeth or probably Diane had called him and explained everything from their point of view. I had sat in front of his desk with its mountain of papers, trinkets, junk, feeling like a ward of the state, a waif someone was generously taking care of. He said he would make every effort to have a substitute by January 10th. So many extra things at this time of year . . . Christmas and New Year's and weddings. I think he wanted to keep talking with me, but I couldn't wait to go. He stood at the door offering his wet hand. I managed, "I appreciate whatever you can do," and left.

I went to my office, closed the door, and sat at my desk. I was angry at myself for assuming the provincials would be intelligent enough to keep my request confidential. Or at least ask me before telling anyone else. How many others had they talked to? And why hadn't they asked me before telling anybody?

"Where in your body do you feel your anger?"

"My legs, my legs." All of sudden I was pounding on my knees with my fists. "Why can't they treat me like an adult? They're all so damn officious. They're all so godawful right." I can't even remember now all that I said.

Iris leaned toward me. "It's all right to express your anger. Use it."

"Use it? I'm afraid I'd kick through their big desk, that big oxy desk they sit behind." I took a deep breath. "Don't they know I'm an adult, every bit as much an adult as they are?"

"You are. Say it out loud as you look directly at them. See them sitting here right now and tell them exactly how you feel."

It was hard to imagine saying to them, "I'm an adult." I had to stand and stretch up to do it: "I'm an adult. I'm every bit as much an adult as you are, as you *think* you are." I said it again and again, louder and louder, until something in me broke open.

I felt lighter. But I'm certainly not going back to talk to them.

I feel lighter right now. I wish I could hang on to this feeling until January 10th.

Wednesday, December 16

I just reread the lines I wrote Monday night. That feeling of relief certainly didn't last.

I am feeling depressed and full of self-pity tonight. I have been dreading this Christmas. Last year was so different. The music for the Masses, the parish parties. I had gone home the weekend between Christmas and New Year's. The entire family had gathered. In many ways, it had been boring, but at least it had been a warm place where I felt I belonged. And when I came back, Bert and I had had a great time ice-skating and then a wonderful fireplace to ourselves at her parents' home. Mark and I had spent an afternoon reading and enjoying the book of Chagall's paintings he had given me. We had spontaneously decided to visit the Jewish Center and sat looking at the large tapestry of Chagall's "Prophet" before going to the little Japanese restaurant nearby.

I'm letting all these memories depress me. I have to stop this self-torture. Right now.

Iris and her husband are leaving for two weeks. I'll have to hold on until January.

Mom told me they planned to celebrate the family Christmas on Sunday, the 27th. I said I had to play the organ for the liturgies that weekend. I told her I wanted to give Jay some time off, but I knew the real reason was that it was easier than going home. I certainly don't feel like an adult there.

Bert is having surgery this Friday. I wish I could be with her, but the last rehearsals for the children's choirs are on that day. The doctor thinks she will be ready to go home within a few days. I certainly hope so. Maybe I could invite her to come here from the hospital.

I would be glad to have her here and to care for her after the surgery. She'll probably decide to go to the infirmary so she won't be a burden to Pat and Evelyn. I'll visit with her while everyone else is at the holiday gathering in the community lounge.

If I could allow myself to do exactly what I want, I'd probably sleep through the days. Read and sleep and watch television. And clear my stuff out of the office when no one else is around.

Friday, December 18

I am still shaking. As soon as I heard Pat's voice when she called from the hospital, I knew something had happened to Bert.

"Incipient cancer cells. They removed her left breast."

I swallowed a wild cry, "What?"

Bert was still in ICU when I arrived. Her whole body, even her heavy brown hair, seemed still to be under the anesthetic. I sat with her mom. Her dad kept pacing, just pacing. We all seemed numb. This wasn't supposed to be. What had happened? Two months from the biopsy. Why had she waited so long? Taking care of everything before she could take time off. So damn conscientious all the time.

Dr. Acher, surprised. But grateful it was detected so soon. Certain, as certain as he could be, they had removed it all. They always say that.

God, I'm angry and I want to cry, and I still can't believe it. I thought if I started to write I could get anchored. All that is coming up is a scream, 'Why?'

For a moment I tried imagining Iris sitting here with me. I need her to help me make sense out of this. But I can't even get quiet enough to stay with the image of Iris.

Bert. Dearest friend. Bert. Bert. All I can do tonight is keep saying your name and seeing your ashen face on the pillow.

Thursday, December 31 These days with Bert have been difficult but very special. I'm glad they are vacation days. I can be with her most of the time.

Bert seems more herself since she is home. But she really isn't herself. She is very weak. She cries often. We both have cried. She is afraid to look at her incision. When Alice came from the infirmary to change the dressing, I saw it. Raw red, puckered, some large sewing pulled tight.

I wish I could talk more freely with Bert about my working with Iris. I know this isn't the time. But I would love to share what I'm learning about my body, about how strange I have felt relating to it. In one way, especially in drawing my breasts, I've realized how much I have ignored this part of my body. And now with Bert's surgery, I realize how maimed and lessened we women can feel with the loss of a breast.

I am coming to understand how much I have to unlearn or re-learn. I'm just beginning. What has happened to Bert makes me realize how important my work with Iris is. I need to re-design my whole life.

Tuesday, January 5

This week whenever I'm alone and quiet, I have been facing the fear of what I'm going to do with all this time beginning next Monday. Six months. To be honest, I haven't been facing it, but when I open this journal, the fear comes right up. I'm afraid I'm going to be alone too much. Everything I've been holding just outside may come rushing in on me.

Also, I don't want to waste the time, putter at some trivial nothings. I can spend hours with little to show for it. I know a part of me would feel better if I were to set a schedule, something specific to do every hour or half hour. That's the way I have been pulling myself through most of these past weeks. I know it's a protective screen, a way to keep all that's churning in me quiet. But Bert's cancer tells me that nothing really stays quiet.

When I talked with Iris yesterday, she suggested for the next week it would be good to break out of my 'time prison.' Do only what I enjoy.

I really want to do what she suggested: do only what I enjoy. Beginning on Monday. This week I have to disengage myself from the parish. I wish I didn't have to be there, but Jay will need help so he can pick up the work. I'm glad he wants the full-time job.

Next week I will try following Iris' suggestion. I can't imagine myself doing only what feels good. I don't think I have ever done that in my life: Ask myself what I would like to do. Every day. No pressures. Sleep when I feel like it. Turn day into night, if I wish. Listen to music, eat an apple, walk, read something I enjoy. Don't put any artificial timelines on anything.

I'm afraid I will feel guilty, lazy.

Tuesday, January 12 There is an urging inside me to get all of the feelings and experiences of this second day of my six months recorded here. Yesterday I slept almost all day. I went from my bed to the couch. I read a half page of Harriet Doerr's book *Stones for Ibarra* and fell asleep. I kept counting on Iris' encouragement to do only what felt good.

Whenever I woke up, I could see Bert's face, pinched and drawn. I wondered whether, even being sick, she could allow herself to do only what felt good. I wish she could. Now and then I could see the choir members looking at me. I don't think they understood my explanation for my six-month leave. It did sound lame when I talked to them.

I felt more rested when I awoke this morning. I am determined to start over, really start over, no matter what. I decided to commit myself to learn to live. Something in me said, 'Open all the windows. Let everything that's waiting out there come in.'

So I did. I opened all the windows in my living room. I heard the heat go on. Mrs. Harris was probably noticing, too, but I didn't care.

Opening all the windows was something I had to do.

I am going to start at the beginning. Let all the vague murky stuff come up. I am going to re-design my life. It sounds melodramatic as I write. But I knew I needed to sit right there in the middle of my living room with the afghan around me and the windows open. I didn't want to hide from anything in me. I wanted to be honest to the bone, to the marrow of my bones.

After I closed the windows, I moved the pillow over and sat in a patch of sun. The January sunlight was a grayed, weak yellow, but it was warm through the glass.

I have been wondering today whether it is possible to feel newborn, to throw out everything I've experienced or learned or wanted or loved and begin all over. As an adult, be totally open, like a new house with room after room and garden and fields and forests beyond which no one has ever walked or lived. All of it to be discovered. And all the past gone.

Mark stopped in on his way to his evening class. I assured him I was going to be all right. He is enjoying his between-semester seminar. I know it would be easy for me to fill my life with his plans, his experiences, his enthusiasm. He is so full of vitality. His presence is still here tonight. But I need to live in my own house with the windows open, moving out all the old dusty drapes and furniture and worn rugs. I need to begin with my bare oak floors.

I watered my plants today. They really are sickly, straggly. Maybe tomorrow I will repot and trim them. Everything here needs a fresh start.

I called Bert. She is finding it difficult to let a substitute teach her classes. She is making sure all the class plans are detailed. Her incision is still draining and painful. I shared my empty house image with her. I could feel her interest, hear a little more life in her voice. As we talked, I remembered a sentence Jung wrote in one of his studies on the different stages in human life: "At the stroke of noon the descent begins."

I wrote the sentence down as soon as we hung up. Is this the 'noon' of my life? Who knows. But I want to feel this important descent, let go of everything I think I have done or been worth or learned, absorbed. What I've done up to now seems gone, forgotten. Nothing. What does it amount to? And ahead? I don't know. But I know I have to put down everything I've learned and from whom I learned it and why they wanted me to live the way I have been. I want to pick up only those things that are true for me.

Sunday, January 17 Today is the first Sunday in nearly 35 years I haven't gone to Mass. I've decided to stop doing everything I do just because I'm 'supposed to.' I sat drinking my coffee slowly one minute after the other until it was too late to go.

The gray wraiths were all around me, taunting me. I wanted them to speak. The more they talked about 'shoulds,' the more I asked, 'Why should I?' The voices said, 'You are supposed to . . . Certainly a Sister should give a good example.' I asked, 'Why?' They said, 'Because you owe it to God.' I asked, 'What about me? What do I owe to me?'

Monday, January 18 Sometimes I think if I could just think all these questions through, read all the books, know exactly what the truth is for each issue that is disturbing me, I would be at peace, free, secure. A year ago I was sure I knew these answers. Ironic.

"Get as quiet as you can, focus your attention on you, not on reading," Iris said today.

How do I know I'm not creating the whole dialogue in me? Is there really an inner voice I can trust? I seem to have a whole tribe shouting at the same time.

I have been practicing following Iris' directive to listen for the dominant feeling.

I've discovered I'm a whirlwind of feelings. I've had to slow down just to catch them. I've noticed I have feelings about how my feet look as I dry them, the tile floor in the kitchen, the dishes in the sink, the radio music, the news report on El Salvador, Mrs. Harris banging the back door of her apartment, the steps of the mailman who brought one bill.

And when I start to sense the feeling under what I am feeling, I find it hard to be honest. One of the things I've noticed today is the *way* I have of thinking. Right away I jump to the negative. I'm critical, expecting the worst, blaming others before I even know the facts. Why do I do this? Where did I learn this way of looking first for what is wrong with something?

Monday, January 25

It was late when I awoke this morning. I didn't have time to record last night's dream before I left to meet with Iris. But I want to write it down so I can return to it often:

I am in a dark prison below ground. The light is coming through very narrow windows high up at the sidewalk level. All women prisoners. We wear shapeless, gunmetal sacks. Guards everywhere. I am washing a laundry sink full of tin forks with my fingers. One of the women prisoners passes behind me and stealthily whispers that I should go to a certain cell.

When I enter the room, a very ascetic-looking man is sitting cross-legged on a cot of boards. His eyes are closed. He is old, with his thin white hair growing down beyond his shoulders and a beard tapering off at his chest. He seems lighted from inside like alabaster. I draw near and sit facing him. He takes my face between his hands, all the while with his eyes closed. Very loving. Then he says, "Follow your light." And immediately I ask, "But how will I know what to do after that?" He says, "Follow your light again. It is always there."

I leave his cell and walk behind a woman who is leaving the prison. She seems to be a visitor. I follow her past the guards, who don't question my leaving. The woman invites me to her home and offers me a bed with wonderful clean soft sheets, and I sleep.

When I wake, I am lying on my side, very close to Mark, fitting into the curves of his body. Both of us are facing the windows. It is morning. Very happy voices of children playing outside come through the open windows. From somewhere in the room a skeletal, tall woman with her hair stretched back tight, severe, walks past the foot of the bed. She glances over her shoulder at us. Her look is one of complete disgust and contempt. She leaves. I don't move. I just lie there listening to the children.

I was embarrassed to share the second part of the dream with Iris. I was telling her how, within a week, I've gone from feeling nothing, only heavy and depressed, to experiencing a geyser of feelings. Feelings under feelings, associations and resentments, old fears, annoyances.

I was going to tell her only the first part of the dream, of my new-found friend. I've been calling him 'Hasid' because he gives me the feeling he belongs to the Hasidic sect of Jewish mystics. I was going to tell her how I want to start dialoguing with him. But I knew that "Follow your light" also meant open the whole dream. So we worked into it.

All of these images are in me. I welcome Hasid and know I want to return to him often. I want to spend more time with the woman who walked so securely out of the prison, a visitor-guide. The young children delight me. They seem to be a promise of new life and laughter. When I think about lying in bed with Mark, I can feel the sexual overtones. I know exactly who the dour figure is. Iris suggested I consider whether this disdainful part of me threw the rabbits against the wall. That Dour One is inside me and has been controlling me. It will take a little doing to befriend her and gentle her strength.

Iris invited me to see that Mark in the dream is a symbol of a part of me I need to integrate more fully. Sexual experiences in dreams are often beautiful symbols of integration, union, she said. I felt freer when she explained that dream dynamics are not tied into our usual social or ethical interpretations and inhibitions.

I understand. What I need to welcome, get closer to, is my own sexuality. I know this dream is telling me that I won't get out of prison until I "follow the light" of my sexuality. I feel very uneasy about this.

Iris has opened some extra time for me tomorrow. I am grateful. She sees this dream as a wonderful gift.

Tuesday, January 26

When I left this morning for the early meeting with Iris, I was still uneasy, even shaking a little as I was driving. Afraid, really, of what might open from the dream. I am finding it hard to admit how deeply inhibited my whole life has been. I know I could pretend to be free like Iris. But I don't want to put another layer around myself so I would look 'right.' Even trying to pretend, I would still be in that prison. Deeper.

Iris seemed so relaxed, centered, as we sat down. I told her how uneasy, how nervous I felt. But I knew I had to talk about the dream, especially the part about lying in bed with Mark. "I feel I'm the Dour One looking at me lying next to him as if we had just had intercourse. I shouldn't be in bed with anyone."

I was trying to breathe. I knew I'd been avoiding the whole thing, not only with Mark, but in myself. "My mind tells me he's an image of a strong part of me I need to love. I tried once to look at, not to mention love, my genitals, as you suggested. I couldn't. And that night I dreamed of the bleeding genitals of the rabbits splattered on my wall. My way of life says, 'Ignore, avoid sexual feelings. They're dangerous. They're wrong for you.' "

"And yet you're here talking to me because it's so painful for you to live ignoring this sexual part of you."

"It is painful, but the Dour part of me is so strong. She's the one who controls me."

"Yes. I think she needs your help. Let me show you something." Iris sensed how heavy I felt. "There's a way to breathe not only to get in touch with how you feel but also to tap into your own good energy source."

She showed me how to inhale deeply as I tilted my pelvis back gently. Then she directed me to tighten my sphincter muscle and send my breath up the spine to the crown of my head. "Hold it there a moment. Tilt your pelvis forward and exhale the breath down the front of your body."

I tried to do it.

"Begin to feel your whole body moving in a free wave from your feet to your head. Let your knees fall apart."

I was shocked and embarrassed. Letting my knees separate as I exhaled was too suggestive. Lewd.

Iris urged me to come through the shocked feeling, not to let it stop me. "You will come to a place where you will feel a shift, feel more power."

I hear Iris' voice as I write: "Let yourself feel alive." It's going to take me awhile to get the feel of this movement.

Wednesday, January 27

Today was like no other day I've known.

Iris had laid out a collection of photographs of the Temple to the Sun in Konarak, India. The Dour One would have been shocked and disgusted. All those arms and legs intertwined. Rows of couples in every posture of intercourse. Row above row, the entire high outside wall of the temple.

I sat there determined to look and to learn. I needed to see those sculptures through the minds of their creators. They were building a temple to honor the sun, to honor Light. Even in stone, the figures seemed filled with light. An inner spirit suffusing the bodies, as Iris invited me to see. The smiles on the faces were serene. Bliss, self-contained, and yet flowing between the couples. Fine-grained passion, giving one another such exquisite ecstasy. Such unashamed pleasure. The children in my dream could certainly have sung and played near this wall.

The whole thing was radical to me. In those three temples, temples within temples, the innermost one was All Light, nothing else. The sculptors were saying we enter the innermost temple by experiencing the Light in the whole of life, beginning with the physical. These figures were not talking, or praying. They were breathing Light.

I have often used the image, "We are temples of God," but I've thought of God as safely locked in a little tabernacle inside me, separate.

These temples were saying something radically different: The whole of life is full of Light. I've been trying to live in the innermost temple, the place of All Light, by ignoring my body, keeping feelings, especially sexual feelings, fearfully in the dark.

It didn't seem radical to Iris. Just natural. She touched one of the white cyclamen blossoms, the plant on the coffee table. "Isn't it strange how we have no difficulty delighting in the beauty of a flower. Probably because the dour parts of us don't see the pistils. The stamens and petals are their genitals."

I looked at the plant. A whole corp of ballet dancers were in wild motion. The same Light living in them.

Finally, I swallowed and plunged: "I need to try to draw my genitals right here. When I'm alone, I get to a point and then some powerful avalanche takes over. It's as though the word 'nasty' or the feeling of being dirty, disgusting pounds in and possesses me. There is nothing I can do."

"Surely you can."

Iris suggested I try to relax and breathe deeply. When I was ready, we went to her large mirror. She sat down next to me. In the beginning I felt nervous, trembling, sitting with her there. Gradually I began to draw.

Iris seemed so natural and at ease. I wish she had been my mother. I saw her eyes as she looked at the drawing. "These fine folds, these opening petals. Your body is beautiful, Marilyn." If her eyes mirrored me, I am indeed beautiful.

I was exhilarated as I drove home. Some lines started. They aren't a poem yet but I need to save them.

A sun dances into every plant
tying root to flower.
To deny the sun in the root is to see a false flower.

A sun dances into my body
in every part a whirling sphere.
Denying the sun dancing in my genitals
is to see a false woman.

Thursday, January 28 This morning I knew I had to return to my own mirror, in my house, in my bathroom. The drawing was easier. I re-enacted yesterday by talking aloud, remembering as much as I could. I concentrated and drew.

The Dour One was there, but I felt stronger as I kept describing outloud the photographs I had seen. With each beginning doubt and feeling of guilt, I focused on seeing Iris' eyes again and hearing her say, "Sexual energy is your life energy."

I thought of my dream, of lying next to Mark. I wondered what he would think if he saw me sitting in front of the mirror. I wondered how he would feel about my poem: "A whirling sphere in every part."

I knew I couldn't share it with him.

I stayed with the process of drawing. But as soon as I felt the heat and began to feel aroused, the old dour part of me became agitated and critical. I became heavy. What am I doing? Is my whole life upside down? How do I know for sure? I became afraid. I stopped.

I am spending too much time with this whole sexual thing.

Friday, January 29 There is no way I can put all of today into words. At the beginning of this month, I had decided that I was going to start living in a whole new unexplored part of my life — house, garden, and field beyond. It was a calm decision at the time. But the prison dream had jarred me, particularly my lying next to Mark. I have been in that bleak prison. Today I broke through the concrete, out, into a totally new continent.

I was calm enough sitting in Iris' living room telling her how difficult it was to feel I was nearing orgasm when I was drawing. In the past when I have been tense at night or when I've felt troubled — especially in the novitiate when I was being corrected publicly so often — I would stimulate myself so I could relax enough to fall asleep. But I have always felt guilty. The pleasure was certainly wrong. I knew it was sinful. Even when I was in high school, I had tortured myself with haunting guilt and always had a sick stomach before Confession. The urge had gotten stronger and stronger until that day at the end of the retreat when I had promised myself that I would never masturbate again.

"I guess the Dour Lady has been with me for a long, long time."

"But you are not liking the control she has on you?"

"No, I don't. Do you ever stimulate yourself?" I was surprised I asked so directly. It was so unlike me.

"Yes, I do."

"You think it's right?"

"I use the power of this energy to make love with myself."

We talked for a while about what making love with oneself means. I was intrigued. For Iris, it's a way of directing the energy, enjoying it, using the energy to become more alive, vital, more genuine. She was so open and natural as she talked about it. I began to sense a whole new way of living. Living with myself lovingly in every part of my life could grow from experiencing this inner power.

This evening I decided it was time to stop hesitating, stop taking mincing steps in my life. It was time, in Iris' words, to experience making love with myself.

I felt I was approaching a frightening chasm. I could run from it again or I could trust Iris and myself.

I did some of the things Iris mentioned. I lighted a large new candle, red-orange, and some sandalwood incense.

This time it was easier to look at myself in the mirror. I felt again the warmth and love of Iris' presence.

When I started to feel my fingers touching and vibrating my genitals, I felt dizzy, spaceless, suspended. I looked into the mirror and into my eyes to steady myself.

"Breathe and relax," I kept saying aloud to myself. I made deep breathing sounds in long waves and tilted my pelvis back and forth as Iris had taught me months ago.

I tried to visualize the energy flowing up my spine. I was expecting to feel heat, but nothing seemed to be happening.

I became anxious. Why was it taking so long? I could feel the mounting urge to stop and run again. But this time I continued to look steadily into my eyes. And continued.

I began to feel the heat. And the moisture. The swelling. And the smell, earthy, as though an animal's fetid cave had opened. Repulsive. The Dour One was about to gag.

I imagined Iris behind me, saw those lighted eyes in the mirror and kept breathing. My legs started to quiver, and I could feel the shift begin in my body. I was nearing orgasm.

I gasped. A primitive naked animal was crawling around on her hands and knees. She had thick black hair, hanging to the ground. Her breasts were loose, pointed. The animal smell came from her. She was wild and wouldn't stop.

I felt my whole face become distorted. My mouth

twisted. Savage. She came directly toward me. She was inside me convulsing my whole body. Something broke loose. A piercing scream, howl, forced its way out of my throat. I could feel this primitive power run through me like fire. Nothing in the universe would frighten this fire. The whole room turned red. I was breathing in great heaves. Gradually, I became calm, rocking myself. The fire was still running through me. I was breathing deeply. And feeling relieved. Grateful. Through the tears I kept saying, "I feel so good, so good." I had never felt so loved, loved from deep inside me. So alive.

Everything seemed more alive. The candle flame moved out in dancing auras, multi-colored. When I turned to the mirror, I looked as though I were about 20 years old. Life inside everything was vibrating. My plants, the lamps. Life was in orgasm.

Or maybe life is in invisible orgasm, expanding all the time.

Saturday, January 30

It's hard to believe yesterday happened. I have to find out more about this whole thing. What about Julian of Norwich, Teresa of Avila and hundreds of other women who learned to concentrate on God and live without sexual feelings? No savage sounds coming out of them. But then, who really knows what went on in them?

I only have to know for myself. "Follow your light." Yes, Hasid, my inner friend, your words ring in me.

Yesterday's stop at the bookstore was a new experience. I'm grateful. I didn't think I had the courage to buy books on sexuality in the open. Something different is alive in me.

I picked up Joan Timmerman's book *The Mardi Gras*

Syndrome. I know I need to read it to understand more how the negating of sexuality happened in Christianity. This author has insights on how natural and God-given pleasure is for everyone. I need this one.

I also found a small book *Tantra*, the ancient ritual. Margo Woods' title *Masturbation, Tantra and Self-Love* in giant capital letters made a bold statement. When I opened the book, I caught a line that surprised me: "My body is the place in which I worship." Just looking at Margo Anand's picture on the jacket of her book *The Art of Sexual Ecstasy* made me recall Iris' comment: "When you allow this energy to move through you in a healthy way, you become more vital."

All the while I was looking and selecting, I kept thinking, 'What will the woman at the counter think?' She looked rather bland.

'It doesn't matter.' This voice had a new tone quality, a hint of the Primal One, maybe. 'Nobody owns you.'

'But if she recognizes me?'

The Primal One would say, 'Tell her you are discovering sexual energy is the key to your true woman power.' I smiled at this voice inside me.

When I put the books on the desk to be checked out, the woman kept her eyes down.

I was relieved my MasterCard didn't say 'Sister.' And sad, too, as I left, that I'm still so fearful.

Monday, February 1

"I waffle," I told Iris. Two mornings, connecting with the new energy felt so right, and I felt alive and healthy all day. But this morning I felt uneasy, and the negative feelings moved in.

Iris made a comparison between sexual experience and eating. Both are natural functions of human life. Her comparison helped. It made the whole experience seem more natural, more a genuine part of real human living.

I was surprised to realize how little I am present while I'm eating. I simply get it over with. I don't take the time to marvel at the power of my body to transform my breakfast orange, absorb it, let it explode like a small furnace in every cell. Food makes it possible for me to live, even to write these lines.

It is intriguing for me to see the parallels between eating and experiencing sexual energy. We change everything with our intention. We can eat naturally to take care of hunger. We can overeat, expecting food to give us a feeling of warmth and security. We can use food, too, to create special ceremonies: wedding cakes, or a tea ceremony, or a farewell supper.

Iris was very clear that I have to know my own body. "No one can tell you how much to eat or when."

Or how often I need or may want to experience sexual energy.

I want to record carefully the similarities. They take hold more deeply in me as I write. I feel, too, as I write the Dour One is learning.

Sexual energy is every bit as much a life-gift as eating and breathing. It feels very new to think of sexual energy as perfectly natural. I need to keep saying to myself, 'It's all one energy from the One Divine Source.'

A new insight for me is the realization that sexual experience and pleasure can be a genuine ritual, alone or with another. I can transform this energy into higher consciousness. It can bring me to ecstasy, creative ecstasy, bring a more refined power to love myself as well as others.

I have been listening to Michael Jones' piano meditation, "After the Rain," as I have been re-reading my notes and writing. A deep sadness is moving into me like a heavy mist from those Irish seas he weaves into his music. So much time has flowed away.

Monday, February 8 On the way home from the meeting with Iris today, I stopped at the stationery store and bought some Craypas and a large pad of drawing paper. I've never worked on 24" by 36" sheets before. They seemed like they would invite larger movements, expanding images. I simply began with a dot in the middle of the sheet, letting the colors choose me and the impulse lead me.

I taped the first drawing to my living room door so I could be with it today. I was fascinated by what unfolded. I found myself drawn back to the piece, looking and looking at it.

Now that I really look at it, I see there is a sharp division in the piece. In fact there is a diagonal split right across and down. One section, the larger, is heavy. It has dark colors, thick, slow-moving lines. The other side is a maze of spirals, multi-colored. My head wants to say, 'See, you aren't integrated.'

Well, I already know that, and drawing lines between the two sections is an obvious, artificial afterthought.

The piece invited me to sit a long time with my inner friend, Hasid. He sees without opening his eyes. I talked with him about the fire of the Primal One. Maybe She's coming through in the colorful spirals. At least a little bit. I finally invited the Dour Lady to join us. She thought the whole thing was kids' stuff, a waste of valuable time. When she's present, I want to tear up the thing. But I'm not letting her direct me.

I promised myself I would work with the Craypas often, every day I could during this time.

Saturday, February 13 I woke this morning knowing I felt different. It seems to have happened quietly during a long dark time. When I finished my morning yoga, I realized I was seeing a new leaf on the ficus plant. It was an exquisite little leaf. Such a refined green. Transparent. I loved it. So small and such a will to live. It has its own knowing, its own personality. We share not only this room, this air; *Wisdoms* would say we share the same Consciousness. I wish I could live seeing each living thing like this: always new.

Whiskers, Mrs. Harris' beloved cat, was looking in at the back porch door. He blended into the snow except for his two green eyes. He looked cold.

When I went to shop for a few things, I really looked at the snowflakes on my coat sleeve. Each had its own being. Two squirrels were leaping over each other in a big oak. Taking time to watch them and delight in them is certainly a different way of seeing, of living, for me.

Evelyn came this afternoon. She wanted me to help her learn a song she would like to teach her fifth-graders. She seemed so emaciated. For a moment I felt I was looking at an X-ray of her. She is so careful, so fearful, so needing to know she would do it correctly. But there is a trapped fire in her. It was good to see her relax a bit with the breathing and the genuine laughing we did. I can't imagine I could have let myself help her that way a few months ago.

Tuesday, February 16

Mark and I went to see "Rain Man." We usually do something to celebrate Valentine Day together. And today is also Mardi Gras.

I have the impression he thinks I'm in my apartment too much, but I also know he senses I'm moving in a new direction. I hear myself talking with more spontaneity and life.

Our after-film sharings are often as rich as the film. Spirited. Mark was taken with Dustin Hoffman's sustained intensity. I appreciated the subtle changes in the younger brother. The way he became more human.

I worked on a poem tonight. It started to happen while we were talking. Our friendship is a gift in my life, clear and good.

I may send Mark a copy tomorrow. I'm not sure. First I have to find out what event in Clare's life these lines reflect. I wonder, with her total love of Francis, if she might have had something like this experience, a strong desire for total intimacy with him. Francis certainly struggled with his desires. According to the legends, he rolled in the bramble bushes to calm his sexual feelings.

Clare to Francis

Light builds a bridge when our eyes meet;
Across it new life dances back and forth.
Light reaches into the earth
for the stained-glass browns of your eyes
And lifts the liquid greens
of all growing things in mine.

Light moves through the intricate veins
down through the genitals to the primal ocean.
There light stops.

Everywhere the fathomless Eye glistens.

It is the word and the image of light moving through the genitals that makes me hesitate to share these lines with Mark. Sometimes the image of having deep physical intercourse with him races through me. I still have a hard time with the dream image I had of lying next to him. But I'm learning with Iris' help to understand these images.

Sunday, February 21

This week I took out my flute and started to play again. It has been a long time, and I realized in the beginning how my breathing was erratic. My flute and I were once close friends, and now we have to spend time to get to know each other again.

Interesting how my flute responds to breath. I could feel the instrument getting warm and coming alive. It took me a little while to re-learn how we had to breathe as one to create real music. Then it is as though my own breath stretches into my flute.

I was thinking how like my own body the flute is. Though my body feels more and more like a cello. I have been doing the beginning exercises in Margo Anand's book on unfolding to sexual ecstasy. I can tell I am releasing more of my fear and choosing for myself. This cello-body has deeper notes and wilder music than I ever dreamed. I'm learning to breathe as one with my body the way a cellist does.

When I first read Thomas Merton's line about having to become what we truly are, I was shocked. I didn't know who I truly was — only what I was forcing myself to be. For so long what I felt underneath all the right appearances was a fear that I wasn't really worth much.

This morning I felt a change in the way I see myself. "What we truly are" is really an outflow of God-consciousness. I had been breathing, breathing up my sexual energy. With each breath, as I stroked my clitoris, I repeated a thought from *Wisdoms*: All of life is a movement into deeper consciousness.

A marvelous bird dipped and crested against the sky, so sure, so trusting. Sheer delight. I felt a light-string was connecting us. Here was Divine Energy experiencing life-in-bird, this bird. I haven't any idea what kind of bird. I do know its spirit was shining.

And here was I. Divine Energy experiencing life-in-me. For a brief moment I was suddenly back long ago at Grandma's, back lying on the rug, looking at the stars. Unable to breathe. I was beginning to lean into that marvelous Sound, close, into the feeling of being inside, in a warm Presence, floating, wave after wave carrying me, moving toward an unending universe where everything is light, is love, is alive. One Sound. One.

I have been homesick for that Sound.

Monday, February 22 – Morning

Since early this morning I have been walking and walking around my apartment, churning inside. I know I have to write my way through this mess. Ever since yesterday morning, with the shining bird leading me close to the magnificent Sound, the Dour One has been stalking around me, grim and accusing. She's right in the back of my head. What about my vow of celibacy? Am I a living lie?

I pulled out all my notes from my readings, but I couldn't sit still long enough to concentrate. Yesterday afternoon and all last evening I kept struggling. Even when I woke in the night, I couldn't turn the tirade off.

Is this primal part of me too primitive, too wild to be of God? How can it be wrong to feel all this new life? Since I've found this vital Energy, I have been so alive, more loving. But am I betraying my vow, myself? Am I losing something worthwhile in leading myself to orgasm?

I went to the kitchen for some coffee. While I was pouring it, I became aware of wanting to be with Hasid, my inner friend. I invited him, with his gentle wisdom, to come and sit with me as I try to sort this out as honestly as I can.

The feeling of the presence of Hasid quiets me for

deep interior dialogue. I am more at home with the primal part of me, and I know I can tame my dour judgments. I need to sort through this flood of feelings — anger, guilt, fear. I could scream.

I vowed 20 years ago not to marry, even more, never to touch my body in a way that would excite sexual feelings. Earlier today, when I was pacing around and asking myself why I made that promise, I felt like kicking the big chair when the words 'for the kingdom of God' came to my mind as the reason for my vow. So trite. Like a formula to be repeated. I thought in the beginning the phrase meant to serve people, to make a gift of my life to God. No one ever really explained why negating sexual feelings was necessary to do that. Celibacy was simply required to enter any community. We were told it was the way to be more dedicated, free of distractions, more devoted to God, even more loved by God. Consecrated. Now I know that kind of thinking encouraged a false sense of superiority in us. I began to think I was special, more spiritual than married women. I wonder how far into me this falsehood has gone.

Being taught as young women that the body isn't holy, that sexual feelings are sinful, was devastating. But we were too conditioned by the training to know it. From grade school on, all the great women they told us about were virgin martyrs or convent women. The women I admired as a student — Amelia Earhart, Willa Cather — never quite matched Therese of Lisieux or Bernadette. That dream, however, the one that showed me those colorless, lifeless women in prison, shocked me. Something is wrong.

Am I too negative? A part of me tells me I must be missing something. The early Christians chose celibacy to replace martyrdom, an heroic sacrifice. Well, that approach is too much like the ancient practice of human sacrifice for me. It creates a violent, monstrous image of God I can no longer accept.

Celibacy by itself doesn't prove anything related to the kingdom of God. Fearful, domineering, and selfish women can be celibate. Celibacy of itself doesn't make them more God-like.

So where am I?

I have pages of notes from my readings about the Israelites needing to separate from the ancient religions that worshipped female gods. The goddess rituals were often a celebration of sexual ecstasy. The Dour One would say orgies.

I just recalled the refined beauty of the Konarak temple. The ecstasy on those faces. How different. I think now we lost something valuable they had. They seemed more at home with the exuberance of life, with the Divine in the whole of life, closer to what I feel with my primal Energy.

The Christian tradition regarding sexuality doesn't make sense for me now. I am grateful for the women theologians who in a scholarly way are now pointing out the destructive interpretation of Eve in the creation myth. All women have been demeaned by the old interpretation. Women's sexuality was interpreted to be evil, a dark power to be feared. The Church Fathers, Augustine, connected sexuality with original sin. Guilt and fear. Guilt and fear and control and suppression all go together to form this 'Dour One' in us. How much longer will this unfounded interpretation be held onto?

Perhaps I made the promise to be celibate too soon. Maybe Dad was right. But if I had waited, I probably would have been married very soon. So I am here . . . but I know I can't live the old interpretations.

I still don't have this together for myself. I'm going to take all of my notes with me to my meeting with Iris. I have to put an end to this wrestling.

Monday, February 22 – Evening

This whole afternoon I have been breathing with a new freedom.

As soon as Iris and I sat down, I plunged into the midst of my questions about my guilt around betraying my vow and the contradiction of feeling more alive as I experience orgasm. "Why are we taught to deny what is natural to show that we love God?"

Iris looked closely at me. "I really have no answer to that question. I have never been able to understand that tradition."

"I thought celibacy had meaning for me once. I knew I was being led from inside me to want to do something significant."

I sat quietly for a moment. "In the beginning I was looking for something wonderful to belong to. A special aura had been created around a community of vowed women. But now I feel sad when I see so many of us working so hard, growing tired, not even knowing we are disappointed. And we keep fitting into old patterns even if they make us ill. All that fear and control to keep everything correct."

As I said this to Iris, the thought of Bert brought tears, and I turned to look at the fire. Strange, I had never taken time to notice the fireplace before. Maybe it hadn't been lit. Little flames were curling around a log right in front. Inside, it was becoming fire. The logs stacked near the side looked dead.

"Many of us are still looking for something to live for, something to be on fire about."

Iris let my words sink into me.

"You are finding that fire now more, it seems to me, in yourself."

I felt defensive. "But what about being faithful to my vow?"

Her comment was true. "It doesn't seem to have helped you very much, has it. Why are you worried about it?"

We watched the fire for a while. Each log had its own way of burning, releasing the sun energy held in it. It does bother me to see even one log smoldering. I want it to burn clean. Like the Primal One in me. She believes in burning. Passionate. I took time to see every piece of wood. No two were burning in the same way.

"Faithful." Iris repeated my word. "To be faithful to itself, the fire must take on its own form. Each log has to find the way the fire wants to come alive in it."

The memory of a short film of Martha Graham returned. Her intensity. Consecration was her word for her lifetime burning dedication to the perfection of the dance. She focused all her being, certainly her primal energy, into her creations. I'd love to live with the fire she has in her dances.

As Iris and I talked, I kept feeling the fire inside me grow stronger. Something started to clear. The vows I made when I entered the community were prompted by a desire to live fully. To be on fire about something worthwhile. Those vows are still true. I am still seeking God. Only, now, my sense of God within life is changing. My image of myself is changing. The old frame doesn't fit. What I promised in the old way of thinking doesn't fit this new sense of God living inside the whole of my living. On fire. Within the shining bird flying in ecstasy. And within me. That Primal Fire inside the vast Sound that warms me whenever I feel the Presence, feel that vibrating, moving Sound.

This insight is totally new. I need to stay with it.

Thursday, February 25 So many changes are happening. Iris is right. The Dour Lady's taunting me into feeling my guilt forces me to face my truth. She helps me open more space inside.

How different I felt this morning as my period started. I have never had severe pain with it, as so many have. Mostly discomfort. When I was teaching, it was an inconvenience, and I was always concerned about the odor.

This morning as I felt the small excitement of the swelling and the movement, the beginning bright red, I was struck by the feeling of life moving through me. Strong, always changing. The old blood on its way, making room for new life, new possibilities. The potential in my life. Life-power, real power to change. I feel in it the invitation to become a woman who creates more genuine life around her.

I was reminded of my mother. To her, the monthly flow was to be kept hidden, a not-nice secret, but she was very kind to me that first morning. She was so attentive that whole week. We had a special connection.

I was grateful to Mom, too, when I was teaching junior high. I can remember twice when a student came in terror at the sudden bleeding. I must tell my mom sometime how much her tender care meant to me.

Sunday, February 28

Bert came yesterday for an overnight. I think she is living with the fear of another tumor. Physically, even with the extra rest and lighter teaching load, she isn't looking that much better. Every now and then I see that fine worry-curtain sweep over her face.

We sat at the kitchen table watching the sky change from deep red to a crocus yellow. The cloud strips seemed alive with the sun behind them.

I wanted to share openly and freely about Iris and what I've been learning, and living. I see more and more how all this vitality relates to health and spirituality. But I was afraid of what Bert's judgment of me would be.

I did bring out Gabrielle Roth's book *Maps To Ecstasy* on dancing and healing. We read some sections and then decided to do the dancing and breathing to the deep pulsing sound of Roth's "Initiation" tape. It was a delight to see Bert enjoy something. The fine vibrations stayed with us into the afternoon.

Last night we lay on the floor in front of the television, which we never got around to turning on. The room was filled with the fragrance of the fresh white hyacinth we picked up at the florist when we came back from our walk.

We took turns reading some of the poems from *The Other Voice*, Adrienne Rich's collection of the voices of women poets from all over the world. We talked very little. The lines were so powerful, the images of women's suffering and strength too strong to absorb quickly.

This morning Pat and Evelyn joined us for brunch. The energy changed with their being here. Even the prayer service Pat had prepared was busier, so many words, than the quiet time Bert and I had earlier. I wonder how long Bert will continue to live with them.

Right now I'm seeing myself in a new way. Disturbing. I regret I didn't have the courage or strong-enough love to share more directly with Bert what I am learning. And I regret I came on so strong with Pat on her statement against groups of women having their own liturgies. It is good learning for me to see how forceful I am when I think I'm right and how fearful when I think I'm going to run into difficulty.

Something else was brewing, too. I seemed far away from all the small talk about community. I kept feeling the concerns were superficial. I wonder whether I'm getting too critical, but so much of the talk was dull, repetitious.

As I'm writing, I'm wondering what would happen if we took the next step into wholeness. What if a whole community of Sisters, what if each one, every woman, was encouraged and free to experience the full vitality of being a woman? Think of the wail and cry all the way to Rome and back.

Would it really be a scandal if we all understood that our sexual energy is a share in God Energy? What a center of life we would become with exploding, creative compassion and freedom. New music, new ways of educating, of healing. It's exciting to think about.

I can't just *think* about this. The next time we are together, I do have to share with Bert.

Monday, February 29 The copy of *Wisdoms* has been lying on my desk for a while. Lately I have been drawn back to it. There was a bright winter sun this morning, so I took the copy with me and sat in the car at the park before driving to Iris' for my appointment. The ducks clustered and paddled slowly in circles in a small pool where the water wasn't frozen.

The page I opened at random was July 15, 1970. I couldn't believe it. The words went deep into me.

> *Now, as the vibrations are being raised and sensitivity increased whole new worlds come tumbling into consciousness. What was dead is now alive, what was non-existent now exists, what was static moves. You feel the movement of Me within.*

I read the passage to Iris. Sometimes, I told her, I feel stretched out of bounds, trying to live into this new way of being. Perhaps I'm trying too hard to think everything through. I want to control everything to make sure I'm right. *Wisdoms* says sink into the deep consciousness.

I was looking at Iris. Large woman that she is, she seemed weightless. There was a hair growing from the side of her chin. With the sun behind her, all the cells of her face and her head and her hair seemed filled with light, moving and setting off glints of color as she moved. She was beautiful. I felt warm. I felt such love for her.

I need to re-read carefully the rest of the lines from that passage:

> *Gone are the old restrictions, in comes what has been repressed. As you move to this vast new Lightness, you leave behind forever the old darkness. My Presence brings wholeness.*

It is really a great gift to feel the old darkness lifting.

Saturday, March 5

I was singing in the car today on the way to the library. I like to take a phrase from *Wisdoms* and create a melody for it. I sing it over and over, sometimes stopping and shifting to a new key until the right melody falls in place. When that happens, it is fastened in my memory.

Today I was playing with a new melody, letting the realization of the meaning of the words from *Wisdoms* take me along: "Let Me be free in you." I just kept breathing, letting every cell open to let Light into me and through me as I sang. The feeling was powerful.

Just how powerful I didn't realize until I got to the parking lot at the mall and followed a young woman. A very tired-looking body. She was trying to balance a heavy bag and was scolding and yanking a little girl along with her. The girl was one stubborn knot.

"Let Me be free in you," came rushing through. I felt utterly out of my skin. I walked up to the mother and offered to carry the bag. Our eyes held, and I could feel the Energy go into action. Finally she relaxed her mouth, put the bag onto my arm, and took the little girl's hand again. We walked together to her car.

Several months ago I would have done nothing, feeling it was none of my business. I would have been angry, would have identified with the little girl, and felt helpless. This Energy is making me more sensitive to people's pains and difficulties.

It isn't easy to write about this. There is the familiar voice of the Dour Lady right behind me: "The whole thing was just an ego trip. What happened was too small even to think about." That voice could really keep me from doing anything.

Sunday, March 6

Mark and I had a strange conversation today. After the symphony this afternoon, I was telling him about the Feuerstein essay I had read on body-positive spirituality. I had hoped to use it as a way of beginning to share with him what has been happening in me. I think I disturbed him. We moved quickly to Church authority and then to 'account-ability,' his word.

In response I turned to a question from an article of Raimundo Panikkar: Is the present Church structure the only possible form? I know Mark respects Panikkar, and I found the question freeing. I don't think Jesus had in mind a priestly class or the suppression of women.

Mark responded sharply. There had to be some way of organizing or any living thing would die.

I started to share what I had read about the early synod in Elvira, Spain. I had never heard of it before I started searching for some understanding of celibacy. I was surprised when I read that they set up the morality code by repressing sexuality rather than encouraging love as a basis.

Mark defended the synod, saying that they were setting up a moral code to separate Christians from the pagan culture of the Romans.

I could feel my anger rising. Their 'moral' code allowed unmarried clergy to claim superior status, special rights to make the decisions and control everybody. "I feel very strongly that the entire repressive patriarchal system has to change."

Mark cut in. "Don't expect it to change in our lifetime."

"Why not? It is changing for me in my lifetime. I find I can tolerate it less and less. I'm simply refusing to give this patriarchal system power over me."

I didn't realize I felt so strongly about the whole thing, and I saw I had touched a live socket somewhere in him. I could feel, as he put on his coat, that he wanted to get away. He wasn't ready to take the conversation any further. It was the first time I ever felt he was putting a distance between us.

Monday, March 7

I rolled up the drawings I have been working on these last two weeks and brought them with me to Iris'. I call them 'my inner revelations' because they let me see what is happening inside me. We spread them out all around the living room. Looking at them laid out in sequence, I could see that they were becoming freer, more colorful. Wild, at times.

Iris sees more in them than I do. We spent time with one from last week. I had started with dark browns. A cave-like hollow at the base of what resembles an old oak.

When I began, everything seemed chaotic inside me. Gradually, circles of colors, yellows and oranges and a loud purple grew out from the cave. In a spontaneous move at the end, I had drawn a tender green shoot in the very center of the darkest point.

Iris kept inviting me back to the unexpected green shoot, reminding me that what happens spontaneously from deep inside needs careful seeing.

I think I'll have this one framed and give it to her for Easter.

Sunday, March 13 I keep going over last week's conversation with Mark. It annoys me that he has not called nor even sent a note to thank me for the symphony. This is not like him, so he must be really disturbed. Or, of course, he may be busy.

As I write, I begin to realize it could have been my new direct way of speaking that bothered him. Or maybe it was threatening since so much of his identity is connected with the present Church structure. Perhaps I should call him. But I'm not going to blame myself and fall back into the old pattern of needing to make everything right with him. It's hard to know what is true. Perhaps sitting here stubbornly is my hurt ego. Maybe calling him to tell him how I feel would be genuine. I think I'll give him space.

I looked in *Wisdoms* for a line I meditated on recently:

> *My voice is being heard and My voice, not that of the mind, will prevail. Simply listen and follow My voice, letting Me become stronger and stronger and the truth will be hidden no longer but will be obvious to all.*

I have a sense that this passage is about the expanding consciousness movement in the whole planet. My concern seems small in comparison. But even with this question about contacting Mark, I do need to listen more deeply. I am learning that when I listen and connect with my deep Self, the insight and the excitement always come.

Monday, March 14

After my meditation time this morning and before I met with Iris — since I didn't want to leave the call hanging — I phoned Mark. I simply told him that I was still uneasy about our time together and asked if we could meet for brunch and talk.

He agreed, but his voice had a little tension in it either because he was embarrassed I called first or because he was in his office and someone was there.

After I called Mark, I sat holding my coffee and absorbing the warmth of the cup. I felt good about following through on the clear feeling that came up.

When I shared what had happened with Iris, she said that there isn't any one right way to respond in a situation, whatever it is. The deep Consciousness in us will guide us each time in a new way.

Wednesday, March 16

Rita called today from the provincial office. When I heard her secretary say Rita wanted to talk to me, I felt some of my old defenses swing in. But when I heard Rita, I liked the tone of her voice. She really wanted to know how I was.

She asked whether I would be willing to substitute as a pastoral minister one day a week, Wednesdays, at the hospice. My first thought was that I must be on the list of the temporarily unemployed. I explained that I wasn't trained in chaplaincy work. She mentioned my parish experience and my theology degree. As if a degree in itself prepared one to help people live through their dying. She added that Miss Fortis would set up a brief orientation for me.

I agreed to go for a few times. If it didn't work out for me, I'd call her back.

She seemed relieved as she thanked me.

Saturday, March 19 Tomorrow Mark and I are going to brunch. I need time with myself first to clarify where I am. Otherwise the brunch will be a gastric nightmare.

I have been gathering my thoughts about our conversation. Why do I suddenly feel so strongly about what is still happening in the Church? Because I am being catapulted into a whole new relationship with the Church? The present setup does violence to us. It contradicts everything I am coming to realize about God, about the Gospels, about women, about spirituality, about body — really, about the whole of life.

The more I learn about how the Church took shape, I am amazed at the labyrinth of this masculinized structure that grew out of imaging God as exclusively male.

I can already feel the argument in me. I don't want to argue. I want to learn more. And I certainly don't want Mark to think that I want to get rid of what Jesus opened for the human family. So much of the *Wisdoms* that I'm meditating on helps me discover what Jesus wanted to awaken in us, that fire of a different consciousness on the earth. And I do want Mark to know this fire in me. I want the heart of the Church more deeply than ever. I'm just beginning to see what the heart of the Church is, "the church beyond the churches" that Bede Griffiths describes in *The Marriage of East and West.*

Perhaps Mark and I could change the whole tone of our meeting by reading aloud the passage of *Wisdoms* I meditated on this morning:

> *I am not just a fact, but a living, growing, glorious movement of consciousness within which vibrates every cell of your body and every atom of your intelligence. Do not hide in the old pattern of deadness, of doing things without life.*

Sunday, March 20

I just watched Mark hurry down the stairs through the rain to his car. He never looked up to give his usual wave.

There's a heavy gray stone in my stomach.

Mark had arrived in a downpour of morning rain. Our greeting was a quick hug, expected, staged I felt.

Before I could suggest that we listen to the lines from *Wisdoms,* he told me he couldn't stay for brunch. The students at the Newman Center needed a priest for their Mass.

He had an invisible thick coat over his raincoat. I tried to 'listen' to his energy, but it was held far down inside.

Mark reached inside his coat, took out his copy of Leonardo Boff's controversial book on the Church, and put it on the coffee table. We had talked about it a year or two ago when it had first come out. I thought it was excellent then. It was a reading Mark used in one of his courses. The corners of some pages were still turned down.

"Here's where I am on the Church." I can see him tapping the book with his finger. "This is the kind of loyal criticism that can bring about change."

I wanted to ask how the Vatican's silencing of Boff differed from the iron controls in a dictatorship. Instead, I told him that I respected Boff and his way of responding.

At the door Mark said he'd call when he got back from New Orleans. Jack had asked him to come down and assist him during Holy Week. That's when the heavy gray stone fell inside me.

I decided to listen to Benjamin Britten's "Four Sea Interludes." The opening bleak feel of the North Sea and the cries of the sea birds in the gray dawn. The swaying sounds of the horns greeting the sun reflecting on the waters. Finally the tympani fearlessly proclaiming for human life in the midst of the storm struggle.

The music is helping me stop chasing Mark's words around inside my head. My imagination can eat away at my good energy.

Monday, March 28 Iris had to cancel our meeting this morning. It gave me a long quiet morning. I slowly took myself deep into my meditation tape on cleansing the energy centers. I did the pelvic breathing and lifted my sexual energy to the most complete orgasm I have ever known. I felt filled with creative vitality, peace, the courage to move through whatever is happening in my relationship with Mark. He's probably in Louisiana already.

Later, a concern about what work I am going to do in the future came up. Nothing is appealing to me right now. No burning commitment. I felt drawn further into the warm feeling of the morning. If nothing is settled by summer, it will be all right. All I need to do now is stay alert, listening, aware of how I feel when certain possibilities come to mind, keeping my antennae out.

Wednesday, March 30

Feet never hide their secrets. They are so human, vulnerable, revealing. They carry the history of a lifetime. And they are so beautiful.

Mrs. Rolland, Sarah, was so restless and anxious today when I was with her. She is moving quickly toward her death and is very fearful.

I asked her whether she would like me to rub her feet. (The administration is wary of the word 'massage.') She nodded her 'yes' without saying anything. As I massaged her feet carefully, she became very quiet and then started to talk about her daughter, how they had never been able to get along.

I began seeing just how much like my mother's feet Sarah's were. I must have been nine or ten when I first noticed my mother's feet. Sweaty, on the earth. She often sat cradling her right foot because of a sharp pain just below the small toes. Her sisters had 'refined' high arches. Hers were not. For a moment I was rubbing her foot.

I asked Sarah what her daughter's name was.

She said, "Bernice," and turned her face toward the window.

I felt she was asking me to leave. So I did.

I'm not sure what I should do at times like this. Do I stay in the room without talking or respect her wish to be alone?

I hear Iris: "There is no one right answer."

I sense now I need to return to Sarah tomorrow. Waiting for next Wednesday is too long a time.

Maundy Thursday, March 31

Bert and I have decided to create our own Holy Week services together.

I was trying in the early afternoon to sense how I might share with Bert some of the things I've learned from meeting with Iris. I thought we might do the Gabrielle Roth breathing and dancing again and then move to Margo Anand's 'streaming,' letting the experience of heightened energy lead us.

But tonight Bert was tired when she came. The last day of classes before the Easter vacation had been draining. She wanted to sit quietly and read the Holy Thursday passages on the washing of the feet from John's Gospel very slowly.

I shared how differently I felt about the washing of the feet since my experience with Sarah. This morning when I returned to Sarah's room, I had brought her a daisy. She had talked and cried about the times when she disappointed her daughter and Bernice disappointed her. She had said her feet felt so warm after I massaged them yesterday, so I had offered to do them again. They were dry and cold.

I offered to massage Bert's feet as she sat on the couch. I could feel her start to relax. She lay very quiet as I brought in the simple casserole I had made. We ate at the coffee table.

Bert left early. She thanked me as we hugged each other, genuine and caring.

I feel a new love for Bert, and I hurt seeing her putting on more weight than is healthy. I wish we could talk more freely, reflecting each other like clear running water. But tonight was not the time to talk with her about what I hoped for.

Good Friday, April 1

This has been a very different Good Friday.

Even when I was small, I couldn't wait for Good Friday to be over. So heavy, dark.

One year when I was in fourth grade, I can remember kneeling without support for three hours because Sister said it could free souls suffering in purgatory. What an image of God I absorbed.

I am grateful for Chardin's essay on his understanding of the cross. The sign of the price of evolution. If the human family is to move to a new level of consciousness, there will always be a struggle, conflict. Change does demand a letting go of the old patterns of thinking.

I spent time today with Paul Reynard's painting of Jesus' death. That Force exploding like a hurricane through his body, his head. Twisting and whirling. His death expanding him into that unending ocean of golden white, white Light. Our own resurrection begins in our conflicts.

Bert brought a piece of cruciform driftwood she had found at the lake recently. It is special for her. After we sat looking at it for a while, I began to sense that this piece of wood appealed to Bert because there was no body. The wood arms gave the impression of folding forward. I noticed Bert was sitting the same way, protecting her scar, hiding her imbalance.

All of a sudden I had a feeling of compassion, of the primal power rushing through me. "Our bodies have known crucifixion. You, with your surgery. Both of us, in the way we have been trained to block our feelings and our energy. We have killed the radiance of our bodies."

Bert looked at me. She seemed stunned. I put my arms around her as she started to shake and then to cry. "I feel so tired all the time, pushing myself along."

"Bert, it's time to transform our wounds." I offered to give her a simple massage, anointing her body.

Her body felt cold and tense. Tremors ran through her as I made long strokes down her legs. At one point she lifted her head and beat with her fists on the couch. "I've been nothing but a workhorse."

We stopped for a while, and I shared my dream of the prison women, wearing their ugly clothes, living in that dark basement. It had affected me deeply.

Later, as I moved my hands in deep circles over her shoulder muscles, I could feel the energy begin to stir. My hands became very hot. When she lay on her back and I placed my hands over her scar, still red and distorted, she murmured, "That feels so good."

A bright red cyclamen blossom was in my eyeline as I finished. I picked it and laid it on the scar. She lifted the blossom and looked at it for a long time, looked at me, smiled, then replaced it on the scar.

I continued to feel the energy flow between us as she dozed. Feelings of gratitude, of mystery, a new sense of the inner meanings of dying and resurrection, whatever came up flowed through me.

Saturday, April 2

It's 2:35 a.m., so it's really Sunday, Easter. Bert stayed over tonight and is sleeping in my room. She wanted the couch, but I insisted she have the bed. I could hear her quiet breathing as I closed the door before I turned on this lamp at the kitchen table.

I have been waking often about this time, staying awake for about an hour, and then returning to a deep sleep until early morning. Tonight I got up to write down some things that happened today.

Through the afternoon and evening, we shared deeply what has been happening in my life. I told Bert about the bleeding rabbits, the Dour Lady, my struggles with drawing my body. I could see all my old fears and questions mirrored in her.

"How can you be so sure what you are doing is right?"

From deep inside I knew it was right to show her the pictures of Konarak. I sensed her feeling change. I paged through this journal, reading parts of it. I shared with her my experience of the Primal One.

Bert's question kept coming back to why Jesus was celibate. Or was he? We took a long time absorbing the Reynard print. Jesus was not afraid of life, moving against accepted patterns. He was not afraid to love and touch and be touched. He certainly didn't emphasize marrying or not marrying. But he did speak intensely about the Living Water within each of us. His message was that the God Spirit was waiting in each of us. As we talked, the significance of the baptismal Easter water as a symbol of new inner life came through in a whole new way, a deeper flow of God-consciousness in each of us.

Bert caught her breath. "Do you think such a vast change is possible?"

I do. I believe we are in front of an enormous shift, probably comparable to the shift from believing the earth was flat. The fear connected with sexuality is deeper and centuries old.

We sat on the floor near the coffee table quietly for a long time. We decided to renew our commitment to what we believe. We lit a new candle. The light kept reflecting in Bert's eyes, little lakes of swimming flames.

Bert plans to spend time building a friendship with her body. She wants to study, think, and read more about what we talked about. I know the urge. I am so pleased with the way she resonated with what I shared. Pleased and delighted. She seemed so much more herself tonight. And she has to move forward in the way that fits her.

My continuing commitment is to love my body more, all aspects of its dynamic energy, develop its sensory powers, catch the nuances of its feeling and their connection with wisdom and self-awareness. I hope to allow myself the high feeling of ecstasy, developing my relationship with the Inner One. I want my body to become a 'light body,' a source of life, radiance, compassion wherever I am.

I am living healthier than I ever have. I feel, too, I am back in the human family. I no longer think of myself as separated, a celibate woman. I am simply searching and finding my way to a life rich in feeling and meaning. I am simply a woman among women.

Easter Sunday, April 3 I was going to write 'magnificent,' but there is no word to catch the experience of the sunrise at the lake this morning. It was too chilly to leave the car, so we sat inside. We had brought coffee and rolls with us. Bert had had orange slices all separated by the time I had reached the kitchen.

We waited for that streak of red fire all along the horizon just before the first green flash, the first second of sun.

Bert read the Scripture passage about the shock of the women at the empty tomb. We felt very close to their experience.

I read from *Wisdoms* just as the full sun rose above the water:

> *In the tender morning feel how the mighty Being which is this earth breathes out and enfolds within itself in great love all creatures which form part of itself, in each of which I am.*
>
> *The massed glory of creation is here; now it is ours to love in freedom and joy, and to enhance. Stretch and be fully yourself, for the earth has awakened and life is flowing fast.*

The two readings blended together. I felt new consciousness rising out of our heaviness and fears. An empty tomb. I felt my heart stretch.

Bert went home about 10:00, and I started to write some lines. A poem was beginning.

In a quiet pause I thought of Mark, and I wondered whether he would call.

I decided to call Mom and Dad. I know they have been worrying about me, but they haven't been intruding into my life.

Dad answered. When he said, "Happy Easter, Marilyn," I could feel his love. Mom picked up the upstairs phone. She seemed hesitant until I started telling them about the sunrise at the lake. I could feel Dad draw back as Mom started to talk about the Easter eggs she and Dad had hid for the grandkids. When I drew Dad back into the conversation, he said the doctor told him he would soon be patched up. His ulcer was healing.

I felt a bit let down when I hung up. Why, I don't know. I must have had some unmet expectations. But I felt real, myself. I wondered whether I could spend a weekend with them without falling back into the old patterns. I'd like to try it soon.

Mark still hasn't called. I'm glad I decided to see the flower exhibit instead of staying home to wait for his call. If he called while I was gone, I hope he will call back. I talked with him in my mind as I moved through the exhilarating abundance of Easter flowers.

I'm still working on the poem from this morning, but it is taking shape. I find so often when I am whirling with deep hurts or anxieties, writing helps me focus. This morning, when I was looking at the lake, I reflected on how different I felt from the time, months ago, when the lake had housed the sea serpent that sucked the life out of everything. And today the lake exploded with life.

Easter Lauds

The lake breathes, inhaling depth.
From that dark velvet womb.

Light flows, filling the water and sky.
Black bobs turn into silver triangular ducks;
washed sands and beer cans swell with light.

Light flows and tree skeletons stretch from within.
Light flows; new today from the First Light,
exhaling memories of continents drifting apart,
of first seed and first fish and first thought.

Light flows and sends the rocks bursting.

Wednesday, April 6

I feel so different these last weeks. I have been breathing, letting my heart expand. I image Light as a powerful ocean lifting refreshing waves into me.

When I went to the hospice this morning, I looked into Celia's eyes as I greeted her at the reception desk. I no longer feel the need for her to stop being so loud and coarse. It doesn't matter. It could be her way of handling all the sadness around her. I now sense a core of goodness in her and want her to expand into full life.

Saturday, April 9

Mark called just before I left this morning. His voice was cheerful, a bit forced. "Shall we have that brunch tomorrow?"

What an odd way to invite someone, almost like an obligation. I said, "Yes, I'd like that."

"Good, I'll come by about 11:00." He hung up. It was

almost as if he had rehearsed what he planned to say.

At the hospice I tried to concentrate while I was breathing with Sarah. She is getting close to her dying and likes to have me come and just hold her hand. I match my breath with hers and let the energy flow between us. It is also a gift for me. I feel very quiet and in harmony with all that is.

Her lips this morning were a bluish gray. The nurse came in regularly.

As soon as I stepped away from Sarah's bed, Mark's call replayed in my head. I felt I was holding all the 'What ifs' at bay.

I have been restless all evening. I tried to read. There was nothing worthwhile on TV. Chopin seemed thin and far away. There was no way I could get quiet enough to meditate into a passage from *Wisdoms.* So I decided to write, pin all this down here.

I am worried, edgy about being with Mark tomorrow. What if he says we're on such different paths that we really can't share? Perhaps the changes in me are threatening him, our conversation on the Church too disturbing.

I'm going to make some tea and take a hot bath. There is nothing I can do about tomorrow until tomorrow.

Sunday, April 10

Tonight I feel in the midst of a wild hurricane. This morning when I walked along the lake, the day seemed calm, promising. A milky light on everything.

The hurricane started while Mark and I were at brunch. Mark sat with his eyes down, studying the coffee in his cup.

I had been telling him about some of my experiences at the hospice. Mark was listening . . . and he wasn't. I stopped.

After a suspended quiet, he looked up. He began by saying that he wanted to tell me something directly. He has become friends, close friends, with the woman who directs the field experience in the ministry program.

A jolt ran down through the center of me.

"You've been staying with her in New Orleans?" The question flew out of my mouth. More like a statement.

Their relationship had started last summer, he said. Someone friendly to be with.

A whirl of questions. Why hadn't he told me this before? How close were they? Intimate? I knew and I didn't want to know.

I tried to push through the sickening feeling and asked whether she were married.

She had left her community several years ago and hadn't married, had her own apartment near the university, Mark answered quietly. My mind continued to spin a whirlpool of images. Somehow everything froze but my mouth. It was saying, "I appreciate your telling me. Certainly you have every right to other friendships." I swallowed. "Would you rather we didn't spend time together?" Everything hung dead still.

"No, no. This doesn't change our relationship at all."

I felt another jolt. What is our relationship if this doesn't change it?

"Some kind of energy just connected Eileen and me." He was so into his relief that at last it was all in the open, I don't think he sensed what I was feeling.

The silence was heavy in the car. I had to get out. I suggested he drop me off at the entrance to the lake park. I would walk home from there.

I walked until my legs ached. I sat finally on the rocks and cried. Just a few tears but they opened my throat. I started to moan, "You idiot," to myself over and over. I kept throwing rocks hard into the water. With each breath

I pushed out, "Damn. I can't believe it. Damn." Something cracked loose. I sank down. I didn't even care that my shoes were in the water.

Monday, April 11 – Morning

Several times in the night I woke up. I dreamed I had slipped or been thrown from a high cliff, arms and legs flailing in the air, and plunged deep into a swift icy river. I worked and worked but couldn't get my face above the water. As I gave a final lunge, I woke up pushing my way from under the blankets.

I wanted to write my head clear last night but I couldn't. When I thought of writing, I couldn't let the pain in because I told myself I should be understanding and mature about the whole thing. And I couldn't be in control because I hurt like a cut so deep it couldn't be felt yet.

This morning I feel empty, a gaping hole in the center of my body. I have an appointment with Iris. I am tempted to tell her nothing about what happened. I feel so inadequate and so betrayed.

I thought Mark and I had a special relationship. Now I feel like a castoff. There is something wrong with me, something lacking. Something Eileen — I find it hard even to think her name — has that is more attractive. I could see the current of excitement in Mark when he talked about her.

I am trying to get ready for my meeting with Iris, trying to get rid of this aching feeling. The ache came up between the lines of *Wisdoms.* The words were dead. I couldn't stay with the passage.

It's time to go. I know if I don't share this with Iris, it will fester in me. And she will sense it anyway. I am struggling with my old self to have myself in control, by myself, so I don't look so weak and jealous.

Jealous. I can't believe I wrote that word. I hate it. I feel sick to think I could be jealous.

Monday, April 11 – Evening I feel as if I have been washed up on the lake shore tonight. As if a high wind has whipped the water through me. Even my bones have been washed.

The tears are starting again. I thought they were all finished when I left Iris.

"Let yourself feel the hurt. All of it. Don't force yourself to try to be understanding and accepting."

I think she must have said it several times. It helped me let go. I'm glad I didn't hide the way I felt. I cried and kept on talking even while I was crying. I'm not sure if what I said in the beginning made sense.

The question Iris asked me helped me see what is happening more clearly: "Why does Mark's friendship with Eileen hurt you so deeply?"

I thought I was special in his life, as he has been in mine. I believed him when he told me how much I meant to him, how much he loved me. Now I feel elbowed aside, a reject. And I feel stupid for having believed him. I'm angry at myself for letting myself be duped, and I'm angry at Mark for saying he loved me. Now I don't know where I am with him.

Iris told me how it important it is to accept what I feel. That I don't need to decide at the moment what I'm going to do.

This afternoon I took a block of wax, something I melted down from old candles, and started to carve. Nothing in particular, just letting the wax absorb the ache, not even fending off my fantasies of Mark with Eileen, of their enjoying the French Quarter together, of her apartment. Sometimes I jabbed the knife deep into the wax, quick jabs. The piece looks like a twisted ape. I think I'll take it and the shavings to the burner in the basement and melt it all down.

Wednesday, April 13 I know I need to become free of Mark. I have to get him out of my mind. I have an image of standing on a bridge with him and then turning and walking away, walking and walking, deliberately not looking back.

But I can't do that. What do I gain trying to hurt him? And I don't want to run away from myself. At this point I can't afford to lock my life shut.

This morning, desperate to lift this heaviness, I turned to *Wisdoms* to get help. These four days have seemed like a nightmare. I haven't wanted to make of God a comfort station. I found these lines, words of the passage that opened a door for me:

> *In the Light of My presence the dark does not exist and as you stay in the Light, the Light remains and the dark is not. 'And there shall be no more tears' — except perhaps tears of joy at the wonder of the process.*

The Inner Teacher in *Wisdoms* spoke directly to me. How futile, when I am full of hurt and jealousy and anger, to try to come through it alone. I can't do it alone.

Yesterday I was ready to tear up every card from Mark, throw out the stones we had collected together, the shells, the Swedish ivy he had given me, the sweater, everything that reminded me of him. Today, whenever any memory comes up or anything reminds me of him, I have been reaching into the dark painful space in me and repeating, "In the Light of My presence, the dark does not exist."

I just keep breathing and sighing. No matter how I feel, I turn to the words and say them deeply, sometimes aloud. I know I'm not alone.

I stopped at the reception desk at the hospice for the list of people I was to visit today. My list is growing. Miss Fortis asked me if I would consider coming one day of the weekend in addition to Wednesdays. Today I was tempted to say yes because I felt each person's pain and fear from within me. It was a relief to be listening and caring for someone else. But I'm not ready to give this time away, though the invitation pleased me.

With Rose, I spoke the *Wisdoms* lines. She asked me to say them again, slowly. We said them together: "In the Light of My Presence the dark does not exist." She squeezed my hand tightly.

Thursday, April 14 Twice as I woke in the night, I kept saying, "In the Light of My Presence the dark does not exist." I listened into the Inner Presence, sometimes close, sometimes vague, until I fell back to sleep.

I was calmer this morning as I did the yoga postures and meditated, lifting my energy, feeling the Primal One surge up. Even as I directed the energy to my heart and throat and head, I felt bruised but quiet.

When I was washing the dishes stacked in the sink from the last several days and thinking about what I was going to do today, I had a surprising image. The whole front of my body filled with light, and from my abdomen a flock of yellow butterflies took flight.

It was unexpected, almost as if for a moment the Primal Light opened the core of me to let in new light.

Friday, April 15

I knew before I picked up the phone it was Mark calling. He wanted to know how I was.

A deluge of feelings. I wanted him to know how much I have been hurting, angry. I didn't want him to think I was jealous, too possessive. I was grateful for his call. I feared if I started to talk, I would start crying again, making a fool of myself.

"I'm really not ready to talk right now."

"When you are, would you give me a call?"

I went back to the poem I had been working on so I wouldn't get on the carousel of replaying the conversation. I'm letting it be for now.

I spent the day with Clare of Assisi. I often like to imagine myself on the little side balcony where she spent her pre-dawn hours. She had a view of the river down below, near the place where Francis and the brothers had their huts.

I began to feel what I imagined must have been moving inside this little Italian woman, so alive, on fire, so committed to Francis and the Beloved Christ of Francis. I wish I knew more about her love. How she lived with her feelings of separation, of being set aside. I wonder how she felt when she learned that his wealthy friend, Jacoba, could bring him fruit and enter his hut to nurse him in his illness. Was Clare jealous?

Clare to Francis

The birds waking in the olive trees say
it is four.
I feel near you on this balcony garden,
free of the walls.
I stand in my aura of bruised purple
lifting the fiery Breath
until the Other does my breathing.

The ellipse of pain opens
with a rush of pure yellow butterflies.
Now everyone and everything quivers
with butterfly light.
I send my breath in the Breath
and let my questions die.

Brother, go free, I shall not keep you.

I feel a good tired tonight. Writing these lines has been cleansing for me.

Sunday, April 17 Sarah died early this afternoon. Bernice and I were with her. Bernice kept holding Sarah's hand almost desperately. Sarah was breathing little short breaths. She suddenly sat upright and spoke: "I must get through the door." When she fell back against the raised pillows, she exhaled a long slow breath. So simple, finally.

I have been thinking tonight about the way people approach dying. Some in relief, some in fear and restlessness. One or two in anger. A few almost as if they weren't there.

Since I started working at the hospice, I've been reading death-and-dying material and life-after-death accounts. I'm coming to realize that dying is as significant and, in some ways more significant, than the experience of being born. It is life changing into freer form.

I hope my dying will be an expanding. But the first moment that I become aware I am dying, I may go numb with fear. I want to be aware so I can focus everything on merging into that full wondrous Sound I keep listening for.

Monday, April 18 When I got out of the car at Iris' this morning, I stopped for a moment to breathe in the sunlight. The air smelled fresh. But I felt heavy-hearted.

As I took off my coat, I asked Iris if we could breathe to some music. I wanted to get the sunlight feeling inside.

"Fine. Choose something you'd like."

A contemporary yet primitive beat of Indian drums filled the room. I could feel the warmth moving and changing me as Iris and I each created our space, keeping the energy flowing between our eyes and letting the music lead.

I shared how much repeating a *Wisdoms* passage over and over like a mantra had been helping me stop the constant swirl of feelings and memories. The dark was still in me, but grayer at least.

I told Iris I didn't know where I was in the process, where I was with Mark. The thought of meeting with him was like the strange feeling of going to a foreign place. With Eileen there as a third presence, my throat would start to ache, and I'd want to get away, fast.

The music and the movement helped me. I was breathing deeply. A long sigh rushed out of me and a flood poured out. How jealous of Eileen I am. How much I hate to admit it. I feel Eileen must have something I don't have. I'm sure she is intelligent, maybe more fun than I am. Maybe she's freer. I was always so on guard. The Dour Lady kept constant watch whenever Mark and I were together. Maybe Eileen doesn't have a Dour Lady. I don't know. Maybe Eileen frees Mark to express love.

I have been thinking about Iris' questioning response, "Is that what you want?"

Do I want freedom to express my love for Mark fully? I had fantasized making love with Mark after the dream in which I had been lying so close to him and the strong Primal One had begun to come alive. It had seemed possible then. It certainly isn't a possibility now. So what do I want? I guess I want to continue to be special to him, to keep my affectionate feelings, to share with him whatever is exciting or disappointing in my life.

Iris' next question helped me focus: "Does your Primal One want you to be special to Mark?"

I felt into that inner dynamic center in me. "No, She threatens him. The freer and more alive I become, I realize what a threat I am to him. She, I, know I'm fooling myself thinking Mark is going to make my life complete."

As I write this, I'm aware that Mark never did complete my life. I spent a lot of time anticipating and reliving our times together. But devoting so much of myself to him didn't prevent last year's dark time, that awful scare with the scissors. This Primal Consciousness must have been shaking me from the roots even then.

Iris offered me several challenging observations: As I continue to grow into who I really am, my relationships with others are bound to change. This could be frightening, lonely, stretching. Her words, as I remember were, "The pain you are feeling over Mark can bring a new turn in your life." I can feel I am being led to be less possessive and less dependent on others.

I have taken most of today to absorb more of my meeting with Iris. I know I am being stretched into becoming more fully the dynamic deep Self I really am.

Tonight I was looking for a passage in *Wisdoms* I had read some time ago. I finally found it. March 14, 1971:

> *It is very salutary to realize you draw all situations to yourself, that everything that comes your way comes for a reason. You can even be thankful for a difficult situation which brought you into My presence.*

I have to be with this passage more. Why didn't my relationship with Mark, as it was, lead me to my deeper self, less selfish, less possessive? Why did it become a difficult situation? Why all this pain? It is true I was over-romanticizing, and my imbalance could very well have drawn this difficult situation. Of course, I could have ended up even more like my mother, more controlling.

Wednesday, April 27 Perhaps I let in the sadness that was all around the hospice yesterday. Or maybe it was writing out all the reports and records of my visits for this month. Even doing the yoga postures and breathing this morning seemed dull.

I sat on the floor and asked myself what was happening. A gush of sadness came up — self-pity, maybe. I saw Mark sitting on the couch as he had done often. His shoes off, relaxing. The way we used to. Perhaps never again. Certainly not with the same feeling. For a moment I could feel myself being sucked back into the dark.

I turned to the Primal One to lift me out of the heavy feelings. As the energy started to move up, vibrating inside my head, a dancer, a liquid form of light, kept changing and flowing and whirling in great ecstasy. The Light kept moving and circling closer and closer, drawing me. All kinds of little specks, sparks were flying off my body as I began to feel as if I were dancing. When we merged in deep stillness every part of my body was in an orgasm of light. And every part of the room — the plants, the rug — were vibrating with light.

I lived all day at the hospice in the after-feel of meditating and lifting my energy, connecting with my deep Self.

I felt particularly attuned to what was happening while

I was with Clarence. He is confused. His knuckles get white when he imagines that his father, who is dead, is coming into the room. I have been massaging his hands and arms until he relaxes. He is so thin I have to be gentle.

When he is out of the confusion, he's a bit coarse with his stream of off-color jokes, which the Dour Lady would certainly not approve. But I think it's his only way of hiding the pain he's in. Besides, I know he appreciates what I'm doing for him. Not disconnecting from him feels so good.

Thursday, April 28

On the way home last night, I stopped at a light. As I waited, I had a flash of a scene. Very vivid. What I believe would be called a waking dream. It returned again today and intrigues me:

I am in the mountains somewhere. The feeling is the same as the one I experience in seeing films of Indians in the Andes. I am standing with a group of people watching in great fear, almost terror.

A young man is coming down a narrow path toward the group. He is tall with long black hair. His hands are tied to a branch behind his back. He is a prisoner, but he walks like the son of a chief. Four men surround him. As the group approaches, the man looks up and at me. His eyes are filled with sadness. I am like stone cracking apart. Somehow, and that doesn't seem clear, either because I was tricked or because I was afraid for myself, I have betrayed him.

I have been trying to shake free of the image. It doesn't make sense to me. I tried the technique of having an inner dialogue with myself as the young woman. I felt into her terror and agony. I asked her how I could have betrayed this man. What part of me is he? She offered no response.

I tried again. This time I moved deeply into the feeling of the young man, inviting him to speak. I asked him how I had betrayed him. What came up amazed me: I have betrayed my strength.

As I'm writing, I know without a doubt that I have been imprisoning my genuine strength. It was my strength, my truth, I have been betraying. I know now that I can no longer follow my dad's way of locking inside myself how I feel, taking care so there are no unpleasant scenes. I can no longer make a prisoner of myself for whatever reasons, even if they seem to be good.

Old patterns are like stone cracking apart.

Friday, April 29 This morning when I woke, I knew it was time to call Mark. I'm at a point where I can be honest with him. I am grateful for the good that came from our relationship, but I am taking a new turn in my life.

The department secretary said Mark was on his way to give a talk in Dayton. "Shall I have him return your call?"

"If he wishes, but it isn't urgent."

After I hung up, I felt I was in a new current. Mark needs to be on his way to Dayton or wherever, and I need to be on mine.

Monday, May 2

Both Jeanne and Andy called yesterday to ask if I was planning to come down for Mother's Day next Sunday.

Iris asked me today what I thought would happen if I were to begin thinking of my mother as an equal, of being with her as though she were an older sister.

I'm taking time to get used to the idea. It's getting easier as I imagine it. I will need to stay close to myself, my Primal Self, should anyone ask embarrassing questions or mention some expectations I can't meet.

Monday, May 9

I told Iris this morning about my visit with my family. I almost wrote 'my visit home.' But I realized very clearly on my way back last night that whenever I am deeply with myself, I am at home, in my home.

I think it was the most pleasant time with my family I have had. Mom kept watching me as I began speaking with her as if she were my older sister. I found myself beginning to use her real name. Emily. At first, she lifted her eyebrows. But I think she liked it when Dad and the others started calling her Emily, too.

Jeanne and I went up to our old room and lay on the bed. She's sorting through a lot of her stuff. Several times she mentioned how alive I looked. She appreciated the idea of calling Mom 'Emily.' I sense it is here to stay.

Sunday, May 15

It was unusually warm today. Bert and I took the two kitchen chairs and sat on my porch in the back. We have been sharing freely since Easter. Today I could feel she wanted to talk about something, so I asked her what it was.

She told me she was concerned about me, about what I would be doing next year. Most contracts are signed by this time of year.

I have been thinking about it, too. I have been toying with just letting things be. I know I could arrange for a few more days a week, maybe even full-time, at the hospice. I even thought of applying for a Clinical Pastoral Education program. But I promised myself I would not take on something or anything just to have a job.

Other people keep asking Bert about me, about what I'm doing. Knowing I don't have to explain to anyone feels so good. Even more, I don't care what they think about me or about what I'm doing. I am freer inside.

I'm looking forward to reading the material Bert said she was going to bring today and forgot. Her description of a woman using music to help people prepare for death touched something in me, as if a tiny desire had sprung alive. It's the first time that has happened about any kind of work in a long time. We'll see.

Tuesday, May 17 The article from Bert came in the mail today. I read it very carefully. Something in me said, 'This is it.' But immediately I had an odd feeling about contacting the provincials, applying for funds to study. It would also mean my leaving this apartment.

I am moved by the description of Dr. Therese Schroeder-Sheker's work. Her intensity attracts me. How she was drawn into creating her approach, using her harp and singing to assist people who are dying. I believe I could do something similar with my flute.

I am impressed by her sensitivity and freedom. I can imagine the provincials frowning when they read about her climbing into bed behind the flailing Russian immigrant, holding the man, rocking him, singing ancient liturgical chants. She birthed him through his death. I find it deeply moving.

I want to learn more about her program. It sounds challenging. The skills she mentions — intuiting the needs of the dying, reading the body signs, and correlating the right music to assist them — are exactly what I have been looking for when I am with the very ill at the hospice.

The article referred only to her research into the music the monks of Cluny created to 'unbind the pain.' I wonder what else she has learned from other cultures. I would enjoy participating in the research and the documentation of the experiences. I like her expression, 'the medicine of sound.' I have a sense that pursuing this is right for me. If it is right, I know I will have the energy to move through whatever I will need to.

Tuesday, May 24 My dreams are pushing me again. Yesterday I was hesitating and questioning whether this work with the dying was right for me. Iris was clear and strong. She helped me draw on my own resources. But inside there must have been some traces of fear. They were gone this morning with the dream:

> *I am in a very large barren field. There are long rows of plowed dirt, but the remnants of what had grown there are dried, brown, dead. A man — dark-skinned, very healthy — and I are working together at the beginning of a row. We have a good feeling between us as we dig a hole to plant a bulb about the size of a*

> *cabbage head. We keep working down the row. I stand up from patting the earth securely around a bulb and look back. All the bulbs are sprouting and growing right in front of our eyes, like a Disney fast-motion film. New, green, with large bright leaves unfolding to a height of eight feet as we watch. We are surprised and excited. As fast as we plant and turn to look, the plants spring up.*

The dream gave me a deep feeling of the rightness of my decision. And I do feel this new strength growing in me.

Saturday, May 28 I decided this morning to do something with the back porch. I have a whole summer to enjoy it. The porch is small, but I have an idea for creating a little garden. The whole space in the rear, as I look down from this second floor, has been depressing. Broken asphalt, garbage cans in the alley way. I hate it. I've been designing a way to block out that view. With some hanging plants and some small potted trees in-between sandboxes, I could make a little garden up here.

Thursday, June 2 As I was writing to the provincials this morning, I knew again how right this decision is for me. I included a copy of the materials. Rita will be responsive if she can see a connection between this program and a new way to be involved in health care. The others will probably question. I will let them know if I am accepted for the program.

I listened to the second side of the tape of Holst's *The Planets*: "Uranus" and "Neptune." The music expands me. Today I can feel "the wonder of the process."

Friday, June 17

I had my hair cut shorter today to look more the way I feel now.

I looked at my clothes in the closet. Iris said casually once, "We choose our clothes and then our clothes shape us."

My clothes are conservative, very right. They look as if they came from a quality store, but I simply select carefully at thrift shops. This summer they all look too wintry. They don't fit how I feel now. Half of them I haven't worn for months. With my height I have to be careful, but I'm looking for looser things, more alive, stronger colors, a little more distinct.

Interesting. I used to share with parish discussion groups the significance of the change of clothes. It is a very human experience to symbolize a change of identity through a change of clothing, like the white garment after adult baptism. It's time to move most of these clothes to the Vincent de Paul Center.

Sunday, July 3

My porch in the back is becoming transformed. I've been accenting the garden with the lake stones that tempt me to bring them home. My hibiscus will be a tree before long. The sheen from the new growths on the potted juniper is a delight. It is turning out to be a miniature island in a small space.

Mrs. Harris came up to see it yesterday. She is thinking

about doing something on the lower porch. It's the first she is venturing into something outside the house since her husband died, a year before I moved here.

Friday, July 8 I need to move slowly with what happened. Yesterday I called the provincial office to tell Elizabeth I had received my letter of acceptance into Dr. Schroeder-Sheker's music program for assisting the dying.

Elizabeth sounded nervous when she told me that she and the others had been discussing the advisability of my continuing full-time at the hospice. There was a great need to have a community member working there. My evaluations have been very good.

I told her I couldn't accept the appointment.

She said they expected an affirmative response from me. I should think it over carefully and call her back.

Monday, July 11 I spent time this weekend in deep quiet, going to the core of me, not wanting to be stubborn, but knowing now how important it is for me to be true to my deep Self.

I opened *Wisdoms* to the following lines.

> *Service to others is from a high state of consciousness; otherwise you simply make moves on the same level and resolve nothing.*

Talking with Iris this morning confirmed my decision: I am certain I cannot accept this appointment. The request to continue at the hospice feels like a request simply to fill an empty position in the old pattern, "making moves at the same level." I am certain Divine Consciousness is urging us — and certainly me — to participate in creating something new within the human family. An entirely new level of consciousness is opening. A new realization of the meaning and reality of death. And how we can lovingly be with each other in the transition. I am certain this is what I am to be about.

After lunch I called Elizabeth and explained my decision. She said I was putting them in a difficult position. I don't believe she heard at all what I was saying. Certainly there was no sense that she shared my excitement. But I can't afford to let her diminish mine.

Monday, July 18

I had a profound experience while meditating and directing my heightened sexual energy to my intuitive center this morning:

> *A swift moving river is flowing toward me. From around a turn a canoe comes very fast. I see first on the flat bottom of the boat strong, large brown bare feet. A woman, tall, dark, is maneuvering the sleek canoe with her feet. She is taller and larger than any woman I have ever seen. A piece of iridescent sapphire material is loosely wound around her waist. She is bare-breasted. She lifts her head, turning from side to side, long hair whipping in the wind. As she moves, everything, trees, grass, come alive on each bank, a rush of green.*

> *She opens her mouth. A primitive full-throated call, three deep notes ring out and out. Suddenly, my throat opens and the Primal One sings the three notes in my voice, a voice I have never heard before, low and exulting.*

I returned to the passage in *Wisdoms* I had read yesterday. It seemed entirely new:

> *In your consciousness of Me you also link with the essence of all. My Presence is so glowing in you that you connect with everything.*

I know this is true. The Primal One is really Divine Consciousness in me. When I am one with Her, with my true self, I am inside the Sound. I am connected with everyone and everything. The Sound is a continuing low hum in me, and when I expand into my deep Self, I can feel it in others, all around me. The Primal One has helped me become more wholesome, genuine, freer, and more loving than I ever hoped to be. And She is me.

Saturday, August 6 I feel so good making the first steps toward moving from this apartment. I have been sitting here at my desk for a while. It has become a special place for me this past year.

I was reading through the opening pages of this journal. I was surprised. It was like meeting a familiar stranger. Jean Sulivan's line from his journal, *Morning Light*, rang inside me: "I was asleep and I didn't know it." I was asleep then. And having nightmares.

I need to spend time pulling all these experiences together for myself. I need to do this, not as an ending, but as a gathering of the insights together so I can move into this new turn in my life-spiral.

I want to share this journal with Iris. I'm not going to touch up anything. I have learned so much about myself, about who I really am in meeting with Iris. She has taught me so many ways I can help myself. I still feel a bit unsure at times. I'm glad she said I could phone or write. I see her widening her eyes, "But always go down inside to the genuine Teacher you have found in yourself."

I have grown to love Iris. I don't think anyone has ever loved or accepted me as she has. She is incredible. I can never thank her enough for her help. I am feeling more of the Energy, more life, more freedom, less fear and pressure — "the wonder of the process."

Sometimes when I just sit quietly in the Presence, breathing, asking, thanking, opening all at the same time, I feel electric. I come close to that feeling during the exultant, expectant moment in Barber's *Adagio for Strings,* that moment when the violins have built and built relentlessly and, at the very peak, that sudden total pulsing silence. I am inside the Sound.

'And there shall be no more tears'
— except perhaps tears of joy
at the wonder of the process.

WISDOMS

Photograph by Jim Harey.

Francis B. Rothluebber is co-director of Colombiere, a center for transforming consciousness, at Idyllwild in the San Jacinto Mountains of Southern California. She is a member and former president of the international community of School Sisters of St. Francis of Milwaukee, Wisconsin, and also a past-president of the national Leadership Conference of Religious Women.

A former teacher and educational administrator, Francis Rothluebber is an experienced facilitator in life-process work, empowering individuals as well as groups across the United States, in Latin America, and in South Africa. Particularly the in-depth sharings of women in workshops and in private dialogue have fused into this work.

The author has also created two audio-cassette series of guided meditations: *From Meditation to Ministry*, a sound basis for effective service; and *Lost Images of God*, an introduction to the feminist dimension of spirituality.

Other LuraMedia Publications

BANKSON, MARJORY ZOET

Braided Streams: *Esther and a Woman's Way of Growing*

Seasons of Friendship: *Naomi and Ruth as a Pattern*

"This Is My Body...": *Creativity, Clay, and Change*

BORTON, JOAN

Drawing from the Women's Well: *Reflections on the Life Passage of Menopause*

CARTLEDGE-HAYES, MARY

To Love Delilah: *Claiming the Women of the Bible*

DARIAN, SHEA

Seven Times the Sun: *Guiding Your Child through the Rhythms of the Day*

DOHERTY, DOROTHY ALBRACHT *and* McNAMARA, MARY COLGAN

Out of the Skin Into the Soul: *The Art of Aging*

DUERK, JUDITH

Circle of Stones: *Woman's Journey to Herself*

I Sit Listening to the Wind: *Woman's Encounter within Herself*

GOODSON, WILLIAM (with Dale J.)

Re-Souled: *Spiritual Awakenings of a Psychiatrist and his Patient in Alcohol Recovery*

JEVNE, RONNA FAY

It All Begins With Hope: *Patients, Caretakers, and the Bereaved Speak Out*

The Voice of Hope: *Heard Across the Heart of Life*

with ALEXANDER LEVITAN

No Time for Nonsense: *Getting Well Against the Odds*

KEIFFER, ANN

Gift of the Dark Angel: *A Woman's Journey through Depression toward Wholeness*

LAIR, CYNTHIA

Feeding the Whole Family: *Down-to-Earth Cookbook and Whole Foods Guide*

LODER, TED

Eavesdropping on the Echoes: *Voices from the Old Testament*

Guerrillas of Grace: *Prayers for the Battle*

Tracks in the Straw: *Tales Spun from the Manger*

Wrestling the Light: *Ache and Awe in the Human-Divine Struggle*

MEYER, RICHARD C.

One Anothering: *Biblical Building Blocks for Small Groups*

NELSON, G. LYNN

Writing & Being: *Taking Back Our Lives through the Power of Language*

O'HALLORAN, SUSAN *and* DELATTRE, SUSAN

The Woman Who Lost Her Heart: *A Tale of Reawakening*

PRICE, H.H.

Blackberry Season: *A Time to Mourn, A Time to Heal*

RAFFA, JEAN BENEDICT

The Bridge to Wholeness: *A Feminine Alternative to the Hero Myth*

Dream Theatres of the Soul: *Empowering the Feminine through Jungian Dreamwork*

ROTHLUEBBER, FRANCIS

Nobody Owns Me: *A Celibate Woman Discovers her Sexual Power*

RUPP, JOYCE

The Star in My Heart: *Experiencing Sophia, Inner Wisdom*

SAURO, JOAN

Whole Earth Meditation: *Ecology for the Spirit*

SCHNEIDER-AKER, KATHERINE

God's Forgotten Daughter: *A Modern Midrash: What If Jesus Had Been A Woman?*

WEEMS, RENITA J.

I Asked for Intimacy: *Stories of Blessings, Betrayals, and Birthings*

Just a Sister Away: *A Womanist Vision of Women's Relationships in the Bible*

LuraMedia, Inc.
7060 Miramar Rd., Suite 104
San Diego, CA 92121

Books for Healing and Hope, Balance and Justice
Call 1-800-FOR-LURA for information.